Edward C Tate

D. L. MOODY

BY CHARLES R. ERDMAN

D. L. Moody: His Message for To-day
Paul's Hymn of Love
Within the Gateways of the Far East
On the Wings of the Morning
The Ruling Elder
An Ideal Student Volunteer
Sunday Afternoons with Railroad Men
Coming to the Communion
The Gospel of John: An Exposition
The Gospel of Matthew
The Gospel of Mark
The General Epistles
The Acts
The Gospel of Luke
The Pastoral Epistle of Paul
The Epistle to the Romans
The Return of Christ
The Work of the Pastor
The Lord We Love
The Spirit of Christ

D. L. Moody

HIS MESSAGE FOR TO-DAY

By
CHARLES R. ERDMAN
*Professor of Practical Theology, Princeton Theological
Seminary, Pastor of the First Presbyterian
Church, Princeton, New Jersey*

NEW YORK   CHICAGO
Fleming H. Revell Company
LONDON   AND   EDINBURGH

Copyright, MCMXXVIII, by
FLEMING H. REVELL COMPANY

New York: 158 Fifth Avenue
Chicago: 851 Cass Street
London: 21 Paternoster Square
Edinburgh: 99 George Street

To
The Memory of One
Whose Ruling Passion Was
the Quest for Souls.

FOREWORD

NEARLY thirty years have passed since the comprehensive *Life of Dwight L. Moody* was prepared by his son, W. R. Moody, and the *Shorter Life*, by his son Paul, and his son-in-law, A. P. Fitt.

These writers are the natural biographers of the great evangelist; and it is gratifying to learn that the elder son is now engaged upon a complete and authoritative account of his father's notable career.

The concise review contained in the following pages at least may serve to call attention to these and other sources of information. Its preparation was requested of the author because of his personal acquaintance with Mr. Moody and in view of his intimate knowledge of Mr. Moody's work and its continuing influence. The task was gladly undertaken because of a conviction that the evangelist's life contains a stimulating message for the present day.

These pages were written before the appearance of the popular and piquant character sketch, *D. L. Moody, a Worker in Souls*, by Gamaliel Bradford. The brief narrative which follows is presented by one in fuller sympathy with the beliefs and methods of Mr. Moody, and it may furnish a helpful background for such more picturesque outlines.

FOREWORD

The substance of this volume was given in the form of lectures delivered on the Smyth Foundation at Columbia Theological Seminary, Decatur, Georgia, in March, 1928. It is a pleasure to acknowledge the honour conferred by the faculty of the seminary in their appointment to this lectureship; and further, it is desired to express deep appreciation for being permitted to present these lectures in this more permanent form.

C. R. E.

Princeton, New Jersey.

CONTENTS

I.	East Northfield	11
II.	The Making of the Man	20
III.	The Sabbath School and Christian Association Worker	31
IV.	The Preparation of the Prophet	38
V.	The Famous Evangelist	44
VI.	American Campaigns	57
VII.	Subsequent Visits to Great Britain	65
VIII.	Finishing His Course	73
IX.	The Transforming Message	81
X.	Methods Which Secured Success	94
XI.	The Gospel in Song	104
XII.	An Unordained Pastor	117
XIII.	A Christian Educator	129
XIV.	The Influence That Abides	141
	Books by D. L. Moody	155
	Other Works Consulted	156

D. L. MOODY

Born, Northfield, Massachusetts, February 5, 1837
Began business career in Boston, 1854
Admitted to church membership, 1856
Removed to Chicago, 1856
Established "North Market Hall" Sunday School, 1858
Married Emma C. Revell, 1862
Organized "Illinois Street Church," 1863
Visited England, 1867
Secured the services of Ira D. Sankey, 1870
Second visit to England, 1872
First extended British campaign, 1873–1875
American evangelistic campaign, 1875–1877
Established Northfield Seminary, 1879
Established Mount Hermon School, 1881
Conducted first Northfield Summer Conference, 1881
Second campaign in Great Britain, 1881–1884
Organized Chicago Bible Institute, 1887
Third tour of Great Britain, 1891
Visited Palestine, 1892
World's Fair evangelistic campaign, Chicago, 1893
Last public service, Kansas City, November 16, 1899
Died, Northfield, December 22, 1899
Glasgow Memorial Service, 1924

I

EAST NORTHFIELD

D. L. MOODY, at the close of his life a generation ago, was the most famous and influential evangelist in the world. He addressed more hearers, prayed and pleaded with more individuals, enlisted more Christian converts, and established more permanent centres of religious activity than any other preacher of modern times.

Elijah ended his career in a whirlwind; this modern prophet worked so furiously, spoke so passionately and swept across Britain and America so frequently, that he seemed to pass all his days in an unceasing cyclone. Yet his inner life was serene; and he was never happier than when in his quiet home surrounded by his family and his friends.

He was a great human. He loved little children and cattle, and the summer skies and the smell of the woods and the song of birds and the sight of growing grain. He could not sing, but there was music in his soul and a merry twinkle in his eye and magic in his touch. His dress was simple, if not careless; his movements were quick and angular; his grammar was sometimes faulty; his manner was abrupt; yet women and scholars and noblemen admired him. His voice was not loud nor pleasing, yet its tones gripped and held multitudes. Experience was his teacher; the Bible was his textbook; he never entered a college classroom; but he fascinated hearers of all degrees of ignorance and culture. He offended some people, slighted others, and irritated many; yet all who knew him believed in his sincerity and rejoiced in his success.

He was shrewd. He made mistakes, but he never repeated them. He could not be cheated in a bargain nor beaten at begging money; and he usually displayed a rare degree of common sense. He was a man among men, and he loved his fellows; but he walked with God, and one day " he was not, for God took him," and thousands wept that they should see his face no more.

Rugged, restless, passionate, fearless; gentle, humble, generous; impelled by a deep conviction of the truth of his message and the reality of his mission; he demonstrated in countless lives the transforming power of Christian faith.

He came from a humble home. He began life as a crude country boy, without education, without money, without friends; but he possessed keen powers of observation, native wit, a sense of humour and an indomitable will. At an early age he began a business career in Boston, and a little later one in Chicago. His interest in Sunday School and Christian Association activities became so intense and absorbing that he soon abandoned his task of selling shoes, and devoted his whole time to saving souls. He was never ordained to the ministry, but in a few years he established a church which has become one of the largest in the land.

While he was still but little known in America, a series of services begun in England developed into an evangelistic campaign which lasted for two years. It carried him into all the chief cities of Great Britain and made him the most conspicuous religious leader of the age.

He was assisted in the labours by Ira D. Sankey,

who conducted the music at the great meetings, sang sacred solos and gave to the masses the Gospel in song.

On his return to America, Mr. Moody was enthusiastically welcomed, and entered upon extended and memorable campaigns in Brooklyn, Philadelphia, New York City, Chicago and Boston. These established an evangelistic career which for a generation continued without interruption. During this time he returned for two extended series of meetings in the British Isles, and he addressed vast audiences in most of the prominent centres of America. His message was Scriptural, his energies were tireless, his methods were wise, and his popularity unfailing.

The power of his personality was felt far beyond the circles of his immediate contacts. By the daily press and in cheap booklets his sermons were widely broadcasted. " Moody and Sankey " hymns were sung in every town and hamlet of the land and in all the countries of the globe. The spirit of religious revival was aroused and stimulated. Many other evangelistic speakers were brought into the field, and the activities of countless churches were strengthened.

In addition to his work as a preacher, his influence was extended and made permanent by the educational institutions he established and by the conferences for Christian workers held under his leadership. It is undoubtedly true, as has been affirmed, that millions derived inspiration and help from his life and work.

The village in which he made his home, East Northfield, Massachusetts, attained unique distinction. It was not only the birthplace and the burial place of this truly famous man, but it became his chosen place of residence, the scene of important and significant activities and the centre of his most abiding influence.

Here D. L. Moody was born, on February 5, 1837. Here, on December 26, 1899, he was laid to rest. To his home, in this place, during a long and strenuous career, he loved to retire and to renew the strength needed for those campaigns which carried him into every part of Great Britain and America. Here, too, he conducted those Summer Bible Conferences, and established the educational institutions which still are extending his influence throughout the whole world.

The village is beautifully situated in northwestern Massachusetts, near the boundaries of New Hampshire and Vermont. Here, through a broad valley, which is flanked by high wooded hills, the eddying currents of the Connecticut sweep southward toward the sea. Along the east bank of the river, on a high plateau, runs the main village street; it is more than a hundred feet in width, and on both sides are double rows of stately elms and maples arching overhead. Back from the street, surrounded by trees and shrubs and attractive gardens, stand the white frame houses, the churches, the postoffice, and the library, which characterize a typical New England town.

Around these scenes cluster legends and traditions of Indian warfare and cruelties, of the perils and privations of early pioneers which are strikingly contrasted with the peace and quiet of present days. Following the main street to the north and east, to the point where it leads out of the village, one may descend a narrow ravine shadowed by evergreens, and may see beside the road a simple monument with the suggestive inscription:

> "Nathaniel Dickenson was
> killed and scalped by the Indians
> at this place April 15, 1747. Aged 48."

However, the place which naturally first attracts the visitor is the one which is associated with an event occurring ninety years later, an event of much more importance to the world, namely, the birth of D. L. Moody.

This " Birthplace," now preserved as a memorial building, stands on a cross-road, high above the main street, and fully a mile from the centre of the old village, in what is now known as East Northfield. This modest farmhouse, with its white paint and its green shutters, with its guardian trees, and its superb view of river and meadow and mountains, was for seventeen years the home of the future evangelist; and there his mother continued to live during all the days of his notable career, until her death in 1896, in her ninety-first year. Recently the house has been thoroughly renovated, and it provides club rooms for the teachers of the Northfield Seminary, a place of rest and recreation. Its main purpose, however, is to perpetuate the memory of Mr. Moody. It contains, among other objects of interest, pictures of him and of his mother, and a large portrait of Charles Haddon Spurgeon, the famous English preacher, presented in recognition of services held by Mr. Moody, in 1892, in Spurgeon's " Metropolitan Tabernacle," London.

Some three hundred yards to the north of the " Birthplace " rises Round Top, a grassy knoll partly screened by sturdy pines and graceful birches. This little hill is sacred as the scene of sunset services held for many years in connection with the Summer Conferences, and still more as the place where Mr. Moody was buried. His grave is on the very crest of the hill. Beside it is the grave of his wife, Emma Revell Moody, a woman whose extraordinary ability and rare grace of character were moulding influences in his career.

As one stands facing the two simple headstones, there spreads northward a panorama of rare beauty, stretching away beyond long reaches of river to the green mountain-tops of New Hampshire and Vermont.

To one who allows his thoughts to dwell upon the significance of the buildings in the near foreground, however, there opens up a vista far more impressive, an expanding vision of a human life, the course and influences of which are vividly pictured by objects clearly in view.

Just at the foot of the hill, fronting on the main road of the village, stands the " Homestead " which was Mr. Moody's residence. It seems but a stone's throw from the place of his burial and from the place of his birth. It was acquired by him in 1875 on his return from the evangelistic campaign in Great Britain which had made him a world figure. His home in Chicago had been destroyed by the Great Fire, and had never been replaced. He had gone to Northfield to visit his mother and to spend a few weeks in preparation for his fall engagements. Here he found a house, nearly adjoining his own birthplace, which was offered for sale, with its rather barren acres of farm land, at a very low price. He purchased this property merely with the thought of spending a few summers there with his family, and of securing for himself rest and recreation in view of the work which was to take him to every part of the land, and frequently abroad.

Yet this supposed scene of seclusion became not only his permanent home, but also the sphere of arduous activities and of abiding service.

A small room, near the entrance of this farmhouse,

was set aside as a "study," where sermons and addresses were prepared. Its walls were covered by crowded cases of books, and its windows afforded wide views of the Connecticut valley. In the dining-room, after every evening service during the Summer Conferences, the leaders gathered to discuss informally various practical topics and to enjoy generous portions of ice cream. To this house visitors came from all lands, and here invitations and delegations were received urging the evangelist to undertake services in every part of the country. It was in the bed-room over the "study" that Mr. Moody died.

From Round Top, looking to the right of the "Homestead," one surveys the rolling campus of the Northfield Seminary. The conception of a Christian school for girls of limited means, who otherwise would be unable to secure an education, was being entertained by Mr. Moody the very year he secured his home in Northfield. Nothing was done, however, until three years later, when he found he could secure the sixteen acres adjoining his own farm. To this, other purchases were added until he controlled over two hundred acres. The land was rather sandy and barren, and was regarded as of little value. At present this campus presents an impressive picture, with its comfortable dormitories, administration building, music hall, school of science, and superb chapel; and forth from these halls hundreds of young women, who have enjoyed all the advantages of a modern education, are going forth into every walk of life and into every quarter of the globe.

Among the buildings visible from Round Top is one which for years was the headquarters of the Colportage Association and office of the *Record of Christian Work* and the school book store, and by it one is reminded of the influence, due to Mr. Moody, of the thousands upon thousands of printed pages which have been sent forth into the world bearing messages of evangelical truth, and stimulating Christian life and service.

The most prominent building, however, which is seen by the observer from Round Top is the great auditorium, which for a generation has been the annual meeting-place of the Northfield Conferences. It was erected in 1894, and has a seating capacity of more than two thousand. Mr. Moody was severely criticized as a visionary when he proposed the erection of such an extensive structure near a small country village, far removed from all the great centres of population. Yet, on the first Sunday it was opened, it was thronged by an audience which not only crowded all the seats, but filled the steps and platform and aisles; and such audiences have gathered for similar services every subsequent summer. It is impossible to imagine how many souls have been given new visions of life and been brought into right relations to God through those historic gatherings of Christians over which Mr. Moody always presided, and which met at his personal invitation and request.

Looking westward and toward the south from Round Top, some five miles distant across the Connecticut valley, one can discern another group of buildings clearly outlined against the purple hills on which they stand. These are the dormitories and the chapel of the Mount Hermon School for Boys, established by Mr. Moody in 1879. It was then, at least, that he acquired two hundred and seventy-five acres on the west bank of the river, and began a work which has resulted in giving a higher Christian education to thousands of youth to whom otherwise such advantages would have been denied. The chapel, built as a memorial to Mr. Moody on the occasion of his sixtieth birthday, stands on a high prominence, and is visible for miles in any direction.

Such, in part, is the picture which lies before one who stands on Round Top. Where would it be possible to secure a vision which opens before the imagination a vista of larger or more permanent influence? Northfield, with its institutions and its associations, is an epitome of an illustrious career; it is in itself a monument to a life of abiding values. Surely such a life must have a vital message for the present day. What were the sources of its power, what was the secret of its strength?

II

THE MAKING OF THE MAN

IF " the boy is the father of the man," then D. L. Moody did not have a particularly promising paternity. He was without doubt a crude, callow, and uncultured youth when, at the age of seventeen, he left his home in Northfield to seek his fortune in Boston. He had attended certain sessions of the village school, but there he had been distinguished more for his pranks and practical jokes than for his pursuit of knowledge. His real school had been that of poverty and privation and hard work. He was the sixth in a family of nine children. Before he was four years of age his mother had been left a widow, utterly destitute and helpless save for her two hands, her courageous heart, and her trust in God.

As a boy he learned what it was to experience hunger and cold and hardship, but also what it was to be generous and cheerful and self-reliant and brave. His home furnished only the barest necessities of life; its library consisted of a family Bible, a catechism and a book of devotions. His horizon was limited to the labours and recreations, to the humble tasks and homely joys of those who were wresting a living from the New England soil.

By way of striking contrast one might think, for instance, of the boyhood and early surroundings of another son of the Bay State who also has become of wide usefulness in the service of the Christian Church.

Bishop William Lawrence, in his recent *Memories of a Happy Life,* pictures to us one who was nurtured amid the comforts and culture and comparative luxury of a Boston home. His parents were persons of wealth and social position. At their summer cottage by the sea, among the neighbours were Prescott and Lowell and Curtis and Longfellow. They entertained Charles Sumner and Oliver Wendell Holmes. Among his own friends were Cabot Lodge and Sturgis Bigelow and Seth Low. As a boy he travelled in Europe, and became familiar with Paris and London. By a study of the classics and history he was prepared for college, and he took a full course at Harvard. He came under the influence of Phillips Brooks, and enjoyed his close personal friendship. He was trained for the ministry at the Divinity School in Boston and at the Theological Seminary in Andover.

Not such is the story of the making of D. L. Moody. No scenes of ease or luxury had a place in his memories of boyhood. No circumstances cast about him an atmosphere of culture. No companions, no reading and no opportunities of travel broadened his horizon far beyond the barriers of his native hills. Yet he did inherit from his father, who was a stone-mason, and from his mother, who was a heroine, and from two centuries of Puritan ancestors, certain gifts and qualities which neither wealth nor culture necessarily insure. Not the least among these was a body of rare physical strength. His muscles were like iron, and his nerves were as steel. For some thirty years he was able to stand a strain equal to which few men of his generation were submitted, and which few men in any age could have endured. Day after day, and night after night, he addressed gatherings of thousands and tens of thousands. He travelled incessantly. He planned and prayed and preached. He pleaded with the impenitent for the salvation of their souls; and he pried money out of the pockets of the rich for the support of his schools. He led his great Summer Conferences and conducted his winter campaigns. He was tireless in his ceaseless labours, and when his co-workers were exhausted he was in fine form for another task.

Possibly it was gift enough from his parents, and possibly it was achievement enough for those early years, to have inherited such physical strength and to have developed that remarkable physique. Yet he had inherited, also, a strong will, a purposeful disposition and a masterful character which made him a natural organizer and leader of men.

He seems also to have inherited that unfailing sense of humour which saved the situation many times in circumstances which were delicate and embarrassing. At least it is true that as a schoolboy he was much more fond of jokes than of books. For instance, his biographers tell of the day when the boy was thrilling an audience with a recital of Mark Antony's oration over the dead body of Cæsar; to make matters more vivid, young Moody had provided a small box to take the place of a coffin for the defunct Roman; in the midst of his oration the speaker struck the lid from the box, and out jumped a captive cat, to the surprise of the assembled citizens and the deep satisfaction of the laughing orator.

The boy had inherited, further, an active mind and a natural independence which led him, at the age of seventeen, to leave his Northfield home and to seek a wider field of adventure in the city of Boston.

After many days of discouragement he was finally

THE MAKING OF THE MAN

given a position in the shoe shop of an uncle, on the two conditions that he would attend Sabbath school and church, and would not try to " run " the business.

The latter condition was a rather difficult one for a youth of D. L. Moody's temperament, but he gave a sincere promise, and developed rapidly into a good salesman and a reliable clerk. His attendance upon divine worship had an even more important issue, for before the end of his two years' stay in Boston he had entered upon a definite religious experience and had become an active member of the Christian Church.

His acceptance of Christ as Saviour and Lord was due to the influence of his Sunday school teacher, Mr. Edward Kimball. This devoted teacher had felt an interest in the ignorant young country lad, and accepted a certain responsibility for his spiritual welfare. He was thus impelled to visit him at his place of business; he found him wrapping up shoes, at the back of the store; somewhat timidly he made his approach; but when he definitely asked the boy whether he would accept Christ as his Master he received a ready and an affirmative response. This act on the part of the youth was intelligent, sincere and serious. It was really the first great turning point of his career.

The deacons of the Mount Vernon Street Church, to whom he applied for admission to membership, may have been wise in their action. After a preliminary examination they kept him waiting for nearly a year that he might be instructed more perfectly in Christian doctrine. However, in the mind of the young man the matter was clear. He knew that he had given himself up to the lordship and leadership of the living Christ, and he wanted to identify himself with the Church and the work of Christ.

He was greatly in need of religious instruction, his knowledge of Christian doctrine was most rudimentary and nebulous; but he never wavered in his decision, and never gave any one reason for doubting his allegiance to his Lord. His religious experience, however, made no difference in his devotion to business or in his desire for success.

Attracted by reports of larger opportunities in Chicago, he started westward to begin his career in that growing, stirring city. Here he at once secured a situation and seemed certain to realize soon his definite dream. This dream was that of acquiring a fortune of one hundred thousand dollars, which would have been much the same as possessing a million dollars today.

His shrewdness, tact, and enterprise made him popular as a clerk, and when a change in his position laid upon him the duties of a travelling salesman, his novel experiences and his widening circle of acquaintances gave him that increasing knowledge of human nature and that ability to deal with men of all kinds and classes which were so invaluable to him in his future work. In a few years he had saved three thousand dollars, and was earning annually a salary of nearly twice that amount.

His business success, however, had not made him unmindful of his religious duties. From his first arrival in Chicago he felt that he must be doing something for Christ.

As he could not preach and had no ability to speak, he rented three or four pews in a church, and filled them every Sunday with young men whom he had invited and brought to the services.

When asking for a Sunday school class, and when

THE MAKING OF THE MAN 25

told that there was more need of scholars than of teachers, he appeared at the head of a band of nineteen young ragamuffins whom he had enlisted in the slums.

Soon, however, he was establishing a Sunday school of his own. It was a crude affair, to be sure, located in a region of saloons, of poverty and vice and crime. It did not follow the exact methods of modern pedagogy; but it did the work. At least it gathered together hundreds of waifs, taught them something of the right ways of living, and brought together large numbers of their parents to hear the Gospel story.

It was then an incident occurred which was instrumental in bringing him to the next great turning-point in his career. Let him tell the story in his own words:

"I never lost sight of Jesus Christ since the first night I met Him in the store in Boston. But for years I was only a nominal Christian, really believing that I could not work for God. No one had ever asked me to do anything.

"I went to Chicago, I hired five pews in a church, and used to go out on the street and pick up young men and fill these pews. I never spoke to those young men about their souls; that was the work of the elders, I thought. After working for some time like that, I started a mission Sabbath school. I thought numbers were everything, and so I worked for numbers. When the attendance ran below one hundred, it troubled me; and when it ran to twelve or fifteen hundred, I was elated. Still none were converted; there was no harvest. Then God opened my eyes.

"There was a class of young ladies in the school who were, without exception, the most frivolous set of girls I ever met. One Sunday the teacher was ill, and I took that class. They laughed in my face, and I felt like opening the door and telling them all to get out and never come back. That week the teacher of the class came into the place where I worked. He was pale, and looked very ill. 'What is the trouble?' I asked. 'I have had another hemorrhage of my lungs. The doctor says I cannot live on Lake Michigan, so I am going to New York State. I suppose I am going home to die.'

"He seemed greatly troubled, and when I asked him the reason, he replied: 'Well, I have never led any of my class to Christ. I really believe I have done the girls more harm than good.' I had never heard any one talk like that before, and it set me thinking. After a while I said: 'Suppose you go and tell them how you feel. I will go with you in a carriage, if you want to go.' He consented, and we started out together. It was one of the best journeys I ever had on earth. We went to the house of one of the girls, called for her, and the teacher talked to her about her soul. There was no laughing then! Tears stood in her eyes before long. After he had explained the way of life, he suggested that we have prayer. He asked me to pray. True, I had never done such a thing in my life as to pray God to convert a young lady there and then. But we prayed, and God answered our prayer. We went to other houses. He would go up-stairs, and be all out of breath, and he would tell the girls what he had come for. It wasn't long before they broke down, and sought salvation.

"When his strength gave out, I took him back to his lodgings. The next day we went out again. At the end of ten days he came to the store with his face literally shining. 'Mr. Moody,' he said, 'the last one of my class has yielded herself to Christ.' I tell you we had a time of rejoicing. He had to leave the next night, so I called his class together that night for a prayer-meeting, and there God kindled a fire in my soul that has never gone out. The height of my ambition had been to be a successful merchant, and, if I had known that meeting was going to take that ambition out of me, I might not have gone. But how many times I have thanked God since, for that meeting! The dying teacher sat in the midst of his class, and talked with them, and read the fourteenth chapter of John. We tried to sing, ' Blest be the tie that binds,' after which we knelt down to pray. I was just rising from my knees, when one of the class began to pray for her dying teacher. Another prayed, and another, and before we rose, the whole class had prayed. As I went out I said to myself: ' O God, let me die rather than lose the blessing I have received tonight! '

" The next morning I went to the depot to say good-bye to that teacher. Just before the train started, one of the class came, and before long, without any pre-arrangement, they were all there. What a meeting that was! We tried to sing, but we broke down. The last we saw of that dying teacher, he was standing on the platform of the car, his finger pointing upward, telling that class to meet him in heaven. I didn't know what this was going to cost me. I was disqualified for business; it had become distasteful to me. I had got a taste of another world, and cared no more for making money. For some days after the great struggle of my life took place. Should I give up business and give myself to Christian work, or should I not? I have never regretted my choice. Oh, the luxury of leading some one out of the darkness of this world into the glorious light and liberty of the Gospel! "

It was this experience which finally led Mr. Moody to give up business and to devote all his time and energies to specifically religious work. This decision, however, must not be regarded as hasty or thoughtless. For a long time he had felt a growing conviction that such was his duty. He was now twenty-four years of age, and ever since his arrival in Chicago he had been devoting an increasing amount of his time and energies to Christian service. That this decision was not easily reached must be clear from the fact that he was successful in business, and well on his way toward amassing a fortune; on the other hand, for his religious work no board or church was responsible, and there was no one to whom he could look for financial support. How definite the conviction of duty had become must be evident from the fact that he resigned his position, and followed what seemed to be the guidance of God, not knowing whither he went.

This decision was the supreme factor in the making of the man. His ancestry and youth had given him a strong body and an alert mind, a love of nature, humour, independence and courage; his experience in business had developed sagacity, a knowledge of men, and a capacity for hard work; and now his life was given a great impelling motive; namely, the desire to bring men into fellowship with Christ. It was this consuming passion for souls which determined his career.

This, then, was the man who in the surprising providence of God was to impress deeply the generation in which he lived; a man of medium height and heavy build; a man not prepossessing in appearance nor impressive in manner, ignorant of the culture of schools, and indifferent to the artificial conventions of society;

a man with small, piercing eyes, and a voice which had enough of nasal twang to betray his Yankee origin; a man of quick, nervous action, and of tireless endurance; a masterful, purposeful man who knew how to meet opposition and to overcome obstacles; a man who seemed born to command and who seldom failed to fulfil that promise of his birth; an impetuous, somewhat imperious man, yet modest in his estimate of himself and tender in his sympathies; a man of kindly humour, of deep convictions and of intense emotions; a man who loved his fellows and hated shams and trusted God; a man whom natural gifts might have made a conspicuous leader in the world of industry or of finance, but who, because of his passion for winning souls, became the greatest single religious force of his generation.

The mention of his impelling motive embodies the first, possibly the supreme, message from his life for the Church of today. It constitutes a call to renewed personal endeavour toward bringing others into the definite experience of a Christian life. Our social sympathies are strong, our religious activities are well organized, our desire for world evangelization is real, but who of us today talks to his neighbours about their relationship to Christ?

One excuse is familiar, and in part valid. Religious convictions are personal and sacred, and to invade the sanctities of another soul is an impertinence and an intrusion. Yet, is this the whole truth? Is our silence due entirely to our solicitude for the rights and welfare of others? May it not be traced to our fear of rebuff, to our memories of inconsistent living, or to the consciousness that our own Christian experience has been lacking in satisfaction, in power and in joy?

There is another excuse more ingenuous and sincere. Dealing with souls is a delicate and difficult task; should we not leave it to others and be content to bear the witness of faithful and loyal lives? Yet is it not true that proficiency comes by practice, and shall one neglect an obvious duty because uncertain of success?

The first attempts of the young Christian worker were so crude and unconventional and absurd that he was known for a time as " crazy Moody." Yet he persevered, and soon became well known both for his boldness and his skill in the fine art of personal evangelism.

" Are you a Christian? " he asked a man in Chicago, as he invariably asked every stranger he met.

" It is none of your business," was the reply.

" Yes, that is my business," he answered.

" Then," said the stranger, " you must be D. L. Moody."

However, sudden surprise and personal conversation are not the only ways of winning souls for Christ. A book may be suggested, or a speaker; an invitation may be given to a place of worship, or to unite with a church. It is not so much a question of method as of motive. Is one's Christian experience real, and is there a desire to share it with others? If so, some way will be found to give expression to that desire. When in any man that desire deepens into a passion, it will mould his character and will shape his career. Such was the experience of Dwight Lyman Moody.

III

THE SABBATH SCHOOL AND CHRISTIAN ASSOCIATION WORKER

THERE are two great modern religious institutions which are deeply indebted to D. L. Moody, and which, on the other hand, were largely instrumental in shaping his career. These are the Sunday school and the Young Men's Christian Association.

Both of these institutions were channels which led him out into active religious service, and to both he gave, for a time at least, the inspiration of a more specific evangelistic purpose.

In the strictest sense, the Sunday school is not a modern institution. The people of God in all ages have been concerned with the religious education of their children. Provision for this was made by the ancient Hebrews. Synagogue schools existed in the time of Christ. The early Church trained its catechumens. During the Middle Ages leaders like Saint Charles Borromeo at Milan were notable for their success in establishing systems of religious instruction for the young. However, we are accustomed to date the modern Sunday school from the work of Robert Raikes, and specifically from his editorial in the *Gloucester Journal* of November, 1783. He did establish a Sabbath school for the neglected children of his city; but his great service was in giving encouragement and publicity to the enterprise in England and throughout the world.

In America the movement became characterized by features which were novel, or on which new emphasis was laid. First, the workers were volunteers and not paid for their services as the teachers of Raikes' schools had been. Secondly, the Bible was the only textbook; and thirdly, the schools were commonly connected with churches, by which they were directed or supported. Nevertheless, it is true that during the earlier years of the life of D. L. Moody the Sabbath school movement, as we now know it, was in its infancy.

While a boy in Northfield, young Moody had attended the school which held its sessions between the morning and afternoon services of the church. He had been brought to Christ by the influences of his Sabbath school teacher in Boston. So, too, when he took up his residence in Chicago, he was at once interested in this form of religious work, and soon established a school of his own.

But in those days Sabbath school methods were rather crude and casual. The movement was somewhat lacking in aim, in organization, and in intelligent leadership. Surely the school which Moody established was sufficiently free from forms and conventions, and at the farthest possible remove from all scientific theories of religious education. Like the schools of Robert Raikes in Gloucester, it was connected with no church, and its pupils, like those in his schools, were drawn from the most neglected elements of the population. Like his schools, also, it became a notable success, and largely influenced the Sunday school movement of the land.

Beginning with something like bedlam and chaos,

MR. AND MRS. MOODY IN 1864 AND 1869

order and discipline were gradually evolved in it. All kinds of methods were tried, and the successful ones retained. The leaders were unfettered by precedent or rule. However, one great purpose was ever clearly in view, that of making Christ real to the scholars and of bringing their lives into submission to His will.

The attendance rapidly increased. Over a thousand members were enrolled. Definite results were evident. Street urchins and potential criminals were changed into useful citizens. Evening meetings for parents were held. Homes were visited and transformed.

Reports of the work began to spread. Mr. Moody was urged to attend Sunday school conventions and to explain his methods and describe his work.

In the wider forms of organized effort he became deeply interested. He was soon appointed a member of the Executive Committee of the State Sunday School Association, and visited every part of Illinois, awakening enthusiasm for the work. Other States called for his aid, and his influence was extended widely.

At that time there was no established system of Sunday school lessons. Each class in every school selected its own Scripture passage to study, and there was no plan or outline or definite purpose in the instruction.

In connection with J. H. Vincent and B. F. Jacobs, Mr. Moody advocated the adoption of some uniform system of lessons. The result was the appointment by the National Sunday School Convention, in 1869, of a committee to arrange what became ultimately the series of International Sunday School Lessons, which for many years proved to be such a blessing to the Christian world.

The supreme service which Mr. Moody rendered to

Sabbath school work, nevertheless, was the emphasis he laid upon its evangelistic aim. He often transformed state conventions into evangelistic campaigns, just as he frequently changed perfunctory teachers into winners of souls. The constant burden of his heart as a Sunday school worker is expressed in the message delivered to the great International Convention in Boston only three years before his death:

"If I had the trumpet of God and could speak to every Sunday school teacher in America, I would plead with each one to lead at least one soul to Christ this year!"

This spirit and this message are needed today. We have vastly improved methods of Sunday school work; we are turning our attention to better equipment; there are other aims which properly are recognized; but are the Christians of America awake to the need of Sunday school work, and are Sunday school workers alive to the need of inspiring in the youth of our land a vital faith in Christ? There are said to be some 27,000,000 children in the United States of Sunday school age who are totally without religious instruction. It is further reported that of our Sunday school scholars not more than one in four becomes a member of a church or a professed follower of Christ. In this generation there must be inspired in our Sunday school forces more of the zeal and the definite purpose which made a successful worker of D. L. Moody over fifty years ago.

The relation of Mr. Moody to the Young Men's Christian Association is quite similar to that which he sustained to the Sunday school movement. This organization had been established by George Williams, of

London, in 1844. Its original purpose was to stimulate the spiritual and religious life of the young men engaged in the dry goods trade in London. Very soon its scope widened. Educational and social features were added to its program with the full approval of its founder; and soon associations were established in other cities of England, and in Paris. The movement was speedily welcomed in Canada and in the United States. Some features of the movement in America were rather distinctive; among these were the erection of large association buildings, the close alliance between the association and the Church, and the emphasis placed upon evangelistic work. No other one man did more than Mr. Moody to establish the movement in this country, or to give direction to its life.

The first association in the United States had been established in Boston a very short time before he reached the city as a friendless boy, and he at once availed himself of its privileges. When he moved to Chicago he found that an association had been organized in that city, but that it was weak and inefficient in its work, and had no building of its own.

As soon as he was established in his brief business career, he led the movement which resulted in the erection of Farwell Hall, then the most beautiful association building in the world. Within four months after its dedication it was burned to the ground; but while it was still burning he began to secure subscriptions which resulted in the erection in its place of a still more magnificent structure. Within three years this second building was destroyed by the great Chicago fire of 1871. It was rebuilt during Mr. Moody's absence on his British evangelistic campaign of 1873-5; but he assisted in raising money for the work, and in

1877 he secured the funds needed to clear the building of debt.

What he did for Chicago in the matter of association buildings, however, is what he did also in large measure for New York and Philadelphia and for cities in all parts of the United States and England.

The second great principle of Association work which Mr. Moody emphasized, and helped to make characteristic of the movement in America, was the inseparable relation which he maintained between the Association and the Church. He insisted that the institution must be an arm of the Church, and not a rival to the Church. He made the organization popular among ministers. He accomplished through it results which otherwise would have been impossible, and united Christians in tasks which separated congregations could not have accomplished. Under the leadership the Association was regarded as a real blessing to all the evangelical churches of the city.

Yet Mr. Moody's chief service to the Y. M. C. A. was his insistence upon its religious and evangelistic purpose. To him was due the success of the historic Noon-Day Prayer Meeting of Chicago; and when he had given up his business, direct evangelistic preaching, in connection with the program of the Association, occupied a considerable portion of his time.

He was a regular attendant upon state and international conventions. He was soon recognized as the leader of Association activities in Chicago. His services in connection with the Christian Commission during the Civil War gave him a national reputation as an Association worker, and in 1879 he was elected president of the International Y. M. C. A. Convention which was held in Baltimore.

For him, however, the first purpose of the Association was to win followers for Christ. It was an organization which gave young men an opportunity of leading their fellow-men into the Christian life. Again and again he made conventions memorable as seasons of spiritual quickening and scenes and sources of religious revival.

In subsequent years the Association has lost much of its evangelical conviction and of its evangelistic fervour. With its superb equipment and its efficient organization it is still accomplishing a great work, but educational and social and athletic features somewhat obscure its religious aim. Its best friends would rejoice if the movement could be reanimated by the spirit which impelled Mr. Moody, and which would make the Association more as it was in his day, a recruiting station for Christian volunteers, a training ground for Christian leaders, a rallying centre for united spiritual campaigns.

IV

THE PREPARATION OF THE PROPHET

DWIGHT LYMAN MOODY was a mighty prophet of God. This does not mean that he was perfect in disposition, a giant in intellect, an ascetic in habits, or that he devoted his time to predicting future events. It does imply that he had a divine message which he delivered with conviction, with clearness and with convincing power.

A prophet is a man who speaks for God; foretelling may be no part of his task. There need be nothing eccentric in his personal appearance or his manner of life; he does not always live in a wilderness or confine his diet to locusts and wild honey; he may be notably human, and live as a man among men. But he must know God and His word, and be empowered by His Spirit. He must know men and love them and speak in a tongue which they can understand.

All these things were true of Mr. Moody. He believed that he knew God; and he believed it with his whole soul. To him God was the most unquestioned of realities, an unfailing Presence, a loving Father.

God must be real to a man who with no backing and no fortune will give up a lucrative position, remarking to a friend:

"I have decided to give God all my time."

"But how are you going to live?" asked his friend.

"God will provide for me if He wishes me to keep on, and I shall keep on until I am obliged to stop."

THE PREPARATION OF THE PROPHET 39

He never stopped; and he seems never to have doubted God, or to have found Him to fail in His loving care.

Therefore prayer was perfectly natural for Mr. Moody. As to its philosophic difficulties and its baffling mysteries he felt no concern. He did not make long prayers. His seasons of private communion were confessedly brief. However, he prayed at all times and in all places and as to all matters which were of the least concern to him or his work.

He taught others to pray. His first really great achievement in Chicago was in connection with the Noon-Day Prayer Meeting at the Christian Association. He went to it when it was a pitiful failure; under his leadership the service became a source of spiritual power throughout the whole region, and with an attendance often of over one thousand.

On his first short visit to England, in 1867, he established a Noon-Day Prayer Meeting at the London Y. M. C. A., which is said to have proved a source of great blessing to the religious life of many. A later visit to Cambridge resulted in the establishment of a similar noon-day meeting, which has continued without interruption for fifty years. To many people the very name of Moody is suggestive of prayer.

A prophet must have a divinely inspired message. Moody found his in the Bible. That was the one book that he knew, but he knew that book; at least he knew its content, and the vital message it has for the hearts and lives of men.

Of most other books he knew but little. His ignorance of art and science and history and music and literature was evident. But he knew the written Word of God, and he knew men. It is estimated that he looked into the countenances of more people than any other man who ever lived, possibly one hundred million; and he is reputed to have prayed and pleaded with seven hundred thousand souls.

A prophet speaks for God to men; and the possession of a divine message and a knowledge of human hearts are essential qualifications of a prophet.

His knowledge of the Bible was acquired slowly, and by diligent effort. He had tried to teach the Book in his mission school, and when this school had developed into a church the Bible was his one textbook; but his addresses were made largely of personal incidents, or of statements of truth he had heard from other speakers. Only gradually did he realize the infinite treasures of the inspired Scriptures.

Among the other influences which resulted in giving to him a prophetic message was his acquaintance with Henry Moorehouse, whom he met in Dublin on his first visit to Great Britain. This young Lancashire auctioneer's assistant had been called of God to be an evangelist. Because of his diminutive stature and his youthful appearance he was known as "The Boy Preacher." With characteristic frankness Mr. Moody tells of his subsequent relations with Moorehouse when the latter came on a visit to America:

"He introduced himself to me, and said he would like to come to Chicago to preach. He didn't look more than seventeen, and I said to myself: 'He can't preach.' . . . I wrote him a cold letter: 'If you come West, call on me.' I thought that would be the last I should hear of him. I got a letter stating that on a certain day he would be in Chicago and would preach for me. I was going to be out of town Thursday and Friday, and I told some of the church officers: 'You might try him. I will announce him to speak Thursday night.' On the Sunday, as I went to the church, I noticed that every one brought a Bible. The morning address was to Christians. I never heard anything like it. He gave chapter and verse to prove every statement. When night came, the church was packed. He preached from John 3:16 the most extraordinary sermon. This heart of mine began to thaw out. I could not keep back the tears. It was like good news from a far country. I just drank it in. For six nights in succession he preached on the one text. The seventh night came, and he went into the pulpit. Every eye was on him, and . . . he preached the seventh sermon from those wonderful words: ' God so loved the world.' If any man gets up in the pulpit and gives out that text today, there is a smile all over my church."

When the meetings were over Mr. Moorehouse said to Mr. Moody:

"You are sailing on the wrong tack. If you will change your course, and learn to preach God's words instead of your own, He will make you a great power for good."

It is said to have been the influence of another English preacher, Dr. Punshon, and particularly his sermon on "Daniel in Babylon," which opened up a new field and led Mr. Moody to preach on the great heroes of the Bible.

It was also to Henry Moorehouse that Mr. Moody owed his practice of giving what were known and widely blessed as "Bible Readings." These consisted in carefully and systematically grouping a series of Scripture texts all relating to a single central truth. Each text was read in order, and illustrated and applied. The effect was cumulative, and very deep impressions were produced.

Mr. Moody also formed an intimate acquaintance with eminent Bible students in England and America. Some books he found to be of special helpfulness, particularly the *Notes on the Pentateuch*, by C. H. M. Of these " notes " Mr. Moody is quoted as saying: " If they could not be replaced, I would rather part with my whole library, excepting my Bible, than with these writings."

Whatever the influences, however, Mr. Moody became a " man of one Book," and his messages were so Scriptural that they came with the authority of one who always was saying in effect: " Thus saith the Lord."

The secret of Mr. Moody's prophetic power lies even deeper still. He trusted in the power of God, he dwelt on the word of God, but he was ever submissive to the will of God. This was the secret of his life. It is an open secret, for the story has been told frequently of that supremely important incident during the same brief visit to England to which reference twice has been made. He heard Henry Varley say: " The world has yet to see what God will do with a man who is fully and wholly consecrated to Him." As recorded by his son, the story thus continues: " He said ' a man,' " thought Moody: " he did not say ' a great man,' nor ' a learned man,' nor ' a rich man,' nor ' a wise man,' nor ' an eloquent man,' nor ' a smart man,' but simply ' a man.' I am a man, and it lies with the man himself whether he will or will not make that entire and full consecration. I will try my utmost to be that man."

How far he succeeded, is the story; it explains the abiding influence of his life.

THE PREPARATION OF THE PROPHET 43

Whenever there is abandonment to the will of God there is an enduement of the Spirit of God. Of this actual experience there are among Christians conflicting statements and explanations. Some persons refer to a " second blessing," some to an " infilling of the Spirit," some to a " baptism for service." Whatever the terms employed, and whatever the subjective state, the essence of the experience is a surrender to the will of God and resultant power from the indwelling Spirit of God.

Mr. Moody was a little impatient with some rather conventional descriptions of such experiences. When asked, one day, whether he had ever experienced a " second blessing," he replied: " Yes, I got it this morning, but lost it again." When Mr. Meyer described his personal experience of a spiritual " infilling " received at Keswick, Mr. Moody said that he never had had an experience of just that kind.

" What was your experience? " a friend asked him.

" Well," he replied, " one day in New York City, walking down Wall Street, I suddenly became overwhelmed by a sense of the love of God. I never had such a feeling before, and it did not leave me. I began preaching with new power, and greater results followed than ever before. I guess that was my spiritual baptism."

He believed in the presence of God, he knew the Word of God, he yielded himself to the will of God, he was empowered by the Spirit of God. No wonder that his service was prophetic, and became a source of blessing to the world.

V

THE FAMOUS EVANGELIST

WHEN, early in June, 1873, Dwight L. Moody left America, intending to spend a few months in England, he was unknown outside certain circles of Sunday school and Christian Association workers; when he returned, after an absence of more than two years, he was the most famous gospel preacher in the world.

Twice before he had visited Great Britain, but his acquaintances and friends there were comparatively few in number. On his first visit, it is true, he had met Henry Moorehouse and Spurgeon and George Müller, and had preached his first sermon on English soil in a little chapel which was under the superintendence of R. C. Morgan, the editor of the London *Christian*.

Then, too, on a second brief visit in 1872, he had formed a friendship with Mr. Pennyfather, of Mildmay, and had conducted, in the north of London, a series of meetings the extraordinary results of which were traced to the intercessions of an invalid woman, who for years had been praying that Mr. Moody might bring a blessing to her church.

However, it may be said that when Mr. Moody arrived in England, he was without friends or fame or funds. Mr. Pennyfather and two other men, who had urged his coming, were dead. His name meant absolutely nothing to the British public, he had no money

THE FAMOUS EVANGELIST

of his own, and no guarantee from any source, even for his expenses.

He brought with him an untrained singer, Ira D. Sankey, to assist in conducting the music at his evangelistic services; and when these two unknown men arrived in Liverpool, no one was expecting them, and no preparations had been made for services of any kind in any place.

Mr. Moody found among his papers an unopened letter which he had carried from New York. It proved to be from a Y. M. C. A. secretary in York, England, inviting him at some time to visit that city. Although assured that it was a bad time of the year, and that religious conditions were such as to make it inadvisable to attempt special meetings, Mr. Moody telegraphed that he would arrive immediately.

York seemed to be the last place in the world for unordained, uneducated Americans to undertake an evangelistic campaign. With its vast cathedral, with its own archbishop, with more clergy and churches and chapels than it ever needed, the little city seemed to offer a hopeless field of labour. The first meeting was held in an obscure Christian Association room, and was attended by but eight people, but it was the beginning of a movement which was soon affecting the religious life of the whole of Great Britain.

Though during the first week the meetings were not well attended, the evangelists were encouraged, and by the second week such crowds began to gather as to tax the various non-conformist chapels which had been opened for the services.

The preaching of Mr. Moody was so direct, so Scriptural and so picturesque in its illustrations, the singing of Mr. Sankey was so novel and so appealing, that a deep interest was awakened throughout the entire city. At the close of the services, at the end of five weeks, some two hundred and fifty persons had professed their faith in Christ.

From York the evangelists went to Sunderland, on the invitation of a Baptist minister, the Rev. Arthur Rees; but his fellow-ministers were either very cold toward the movement or actually opposed to it. This was not surprising. The evangelists were plain men without position or prestige or culture. They were not clergymen, nor even ministers. Their methods were strange. The preaching of Mr. Moody was not in accordance with their accepted standards, and the singing of Mr. Sankey was "not worship." The attendance at the meetings increased in number, but the opposition likewise increased.

"We can never go on in this way," Mr. Moody is reported as saying. "It is easier fighting the devil than fighting the ministers."

Nevertheless, the interest deepened. It became necessary to employ Victoria Hall, one of the largest halls in the north of England. The Y. M. C. A. workers were among the first to co-operate, and one of them afterwards reported: "The people of Sunderland warmly supported the movement in spite of their spiritual advisers; there was a tremendous work of grace when measured by its immediate effects, but far greater in its consequences, after the evangelists were gone away."

Newcastle-on-Tyne was next visited. "Here Mr. Moody," writes one biographer, "set himself down before Great Britain with the deliberate determination of conquering its prejudices against himself, and breaking his way into the confidence of its people, in order to bring them the message he bore from God. 'We have not done much in York and Sunderland,' said he, 'because the ministers opposed us; but we are going to stay in Newcastle till we make an impression, and live down the prejudices of good people who do not understand us.'"

Whether or not this was Mr. Moody's expressed purpose, such was indeed the result of his stay in Newcastle. One after another, the leading ministers joined hands with the evangelists, and even some of the clergy of the Established Church expressed their sympathy with the movement. Converts by the hundreds were received into all the evangelical churches. All the north of England was reached and aroused, and tidings of the spiritual awakening were published by the press, and sent by letter and telegraph all over Great Britain as the most remarkable current news.

One interesting fact in connection with the Newcastle meetings is that at this time a book of "Moody and Sankey Hymns" first came into being. The evangelists had been using a book by Philip Phillips entitled *Hallowed Songs*. Mr. Sankey offered to the publishers to supply a dozen of the hymns which he had brought from America and which had become very popular in the meetings, in case the publishers would print them in the back of their own book. When this offer was not accepted and similar offers were declined, Mr. R. C. Morgan, editor of the *Christian*, who had come from London to report the meetings, expressed his willingness to take the hymns and publish them in small pamphlet form.

"So I cut from my scrap-book twenty-three pieces," wrote Mr. Sankey, "rolled them up and wrote on them

the words, 'Sacred Songs and Solos, sung by Ira D. Sankey at the meetings of Mr. Moody, of Chicago.'"
From itme to time other songs were added, and a few months later an edition of "words only" was published and sold for a penny. The popularity of the book was widely extended by advertisement in the *Christian,* and the songs were soon known in every part of the land.

The surest proof of Mr. Moody's success in Newcastle is the fact that he was invited to go for a series of services in Edinburgh.

It must not be imagined that this invitation to the centre of religious life and thought in Scotland was lightly given. The Scots have always prided themselves on their knowledge of theology. With them doctrinal discussions are supposed to have supplied largely the place of popular amusements among other peoples. Their sermons were solemn, and church-going was an awesome and dire duty.

Then, too, there was much that was suspicious about these strange American religious adventurers. Mr. Moody had the stamp of no college upon him, and he came with the endorsement of no church or denomination or body of divines. His grammar was not always perfect, his theology a little difficult to classify, and his illustrations were often humourous and sometimes appalling.

His companion was even more questionable. To say the least, "he did not sing according to Scottish tradition." He sang but few Psalms, and these were not in the accepted versions. Much of his music was unpleasantly suggestive of places other than churches. However, the chief abomination was the cabinet organ, the "kist fu' o'whistles" with which he accompanied

THE FAMOUS EVANGELIST

his voice; such instruments had been kept out of the Scotch sanctuary for three centuries.

However, reports from Newcastle had aroused such interest, and personal investigations resulted so favourably, that at last the bold venture was made and the invitation was extended. We are told that when Dr. Horatius Bonar had returned with a glowing report in favour of the evangelists he was instantly asked:

"But what about Sankey's organ?"

"Ah, well," replied Dr. Bonar naïvely, "it is a very little one!"

The success of the meetings was immediate and sustained. On the day after the arrival of the evangelists the Music Hall, seating two thousand people, was thronged to hear them. Every evening the Free Church Assembly Hall, the largest public building in Edinburgh, and the Assembly Hall of the Established Church, were crowded with eager listeners. The secular press gave great space in every edition to reports of the meetings. There was but one general theme of conversation throughout the city. People came from distant towns to attend the meetings, and chosen messengers went from Edinburgh to all parts of Scotland, holding services and spreading the spirit of revival.

Noon-day meetings were held for prayer, large numbers crowded into the inquiry rooms at the close of the evening services, and hundreds confessed conversion. A call to prayer, signed by the leading ministers of Edinburgh, was sent to every church in Scotland, and the whole country was stirred as it had not been for generations.

When the work had been in progress only five weeks, the *British Evangelist,* published in London, reported as follows:

"There has been a great work of grace in Edinburgh under the preaching of Mr. Moody and the singing of Mr. Sankey. Ten thousand souls have heard them. No one place in the city can be got to contain the crowds. The impression has been marked and general. Hundreds have been conversed with, anxious about salvation, at the close of the preachings, and hundreds leave nightly with anxiety in their hearts. All evangelical ministers and Christian workers of all churches are co-operating with them. Two, three, and four places are sometimes opened simultaneously to contain the crowds. A multitude assembles at noon to pray, and the power of the Spirit there is very great; and so deep is the feeling that half the assembly are sometimes in tears, weeping for very joy of the Holy Ghost. We have had the beginning of what promises to be deep, spiritual, solid, and permanent."

This promise was abundantly fulfilled. Not only Edinburgh but the whole of Scotland was moved and, according to competent judges, moved as never before. Thousands of Christians were aroused to more active service and inspired to more consistent living. Some seventeen hundred new converts were reported; Dr. Bonar declared "that there was scarcely a Christian household in all Edinburgh in which there were not one or more persons converted during the revival." These converts were divided into classes and placed under the care of the pastors to whose congregations they properly belonged.

After the close of a subsequent mission in Glasgow, Mr. Moody returned for a "farewell meeting" at Edinburgh. The service was held in the open air, in the fields on the slope of Arthur's Seat, as no building would have been adequate to accommodate the vast

THE FAMOUS EVANGELIST

throngs who assembled. It seemed that the whole city turned out to bid the evangelist Godspeed, and Mr. Moody is said to have addressed at this time more than twenty thousand people.

One notable effect of the meetings, as recorded by the *British Evangelist,* was the spirit of Christian unity which was produced: " It is a charming sight to look back over the past week and think of men whom it appeared were for all time to come in religious antagonism because of their controversial differences, sitting side by side on the same platform lovingly co-operating with those American brethren and with one another for the conversion of souls. All old things seemed to have passed away, and all things had become new. There has been such a commingling of ministers and Christians of all the churches—all sectarian thoughts and feelings being buried—as has never been witnessed in this city since the first breaking up of the Church of Scotland, more than one hundred and forty years ago. What all the ministers and people of Scotland were unable to achieve—a union of Christians on a doctrinal basis—God has effected, as it were, at once, on the basis of the inner life by the singing of a few simple hymns and the simple preaching of the gospel."

Glasgow became the scene and centre of similar religious revival. Among the characteristic features of this mission might be mentioned the preparatory meetings, which were held nightly for a period of weeks before the arrival of the evangelists; also, the great chorus choir assembled to help in the service of song; and further, the novel services of specific classes. At one of these meetings for young men, " one hundred and one " took a definite stand for Christ. Most notable of all were the permanent results of the meetings, not only in changed lives, but in the establishment of permanent institutions, which for more than half a century have continued to carry on their philanthropic and evangelistic work. At the last meeting, advertised for the Crystal Palace, when the auditorium had been filled with a throng of six or seven thousand, the crowds outside the building were so much larger that Mr. Moody decided to speak in the open air, and thus addressed some thirty thousand auditors.

Invitations had come to the evangelists from every part of the land, and the summer months were devoted to meetings in all the principal cities of Scotland, before heeding the urgent appeal to undertake work in Ireland. Beginning with Belfast and closing the mission in Dublin, the American evangelists awakened a deep interest throughout the whole north of Ireland, and the meetings and results were similar to those in Scotland.

The crowds which attempted to attend the meetings in Belfast were often three and four times the capacity of the buildings employed. It was necessary to hold special meetings strictly limited to certain classes, men or women, teachers or children; and Mr. Moody held a very unusual number of outdoor meetings. The last meeting, held for new converts exclusively, to which admission was only by ticket, was attended by more than two thousand persons.

At Londonderry the throngs were largely augmented by excursionists who arrived on special trains run from many surrounding districts. According to the report, "a great harvest of souls was gathered in five short weeks."

In Dublin, in spite of its comparatively small population of Protestants, the Irish mission reached its

THE FAMOUS EVANGELIST

climax. At Mr. Moody's urgent request the great Exhibition Palace was engaged for the meetings. In further preparation weeks had been spent in prayer, and thousands of tracts describing the revival in Scotland had been distributed. One feature of the meetings was the large number of ministers of all evangelical denominations who co-operated.

In the matter of converts the line of separation between Protestants and Catholics was very frequently crossed. Mr. Moody always had the wisdom and grace to give no offence to Catholics, and when surprise was expressed by someone at the large number of Catholic converts, he asked characteristically: " Why should we distinguish between different kinds of converts. Are we not all one in Christ? "

The mission closed with a conference lasting for three days, attended by Christian workers from all parts of Ireland, including some eight hundred ministers of all evangelical denominations. The second day some two thousand persons were present who during the previous six months had professed their faith in Christ.

In his farewell address Mr. Moody disclaimed any personal credit for the great results of the meetings, and fixed the thought of his hearers upon their unseen Lord. When the evangelists left Dublin it was said that they " were laden with more heartfelt benedictions than ever went out of Ireland before with any two men."

On their return to England the evangelists were eagerly welcomed to Manchester, Sheffield, Birmingham and Liverpool.

In the first of these cities the success was so immediate that within a week it was said: " Manchester is now on fire. The most difficult of all English cities to kindle by anything but politics is now fairly ablaze, and the flames are breaking out in every direction."

The desire to visibly express the growing feeling of unity led to the erection of a Y. M. C. A. building which cost some $150,000. The meetings at Manchester were said to have taken less of the joyful character which had marked those in Scotland and Ireland.

At Sheffield the meetings began with a most impressive "watch-night meeting" during the last hours of the closing year, 1874. However, there was at first some disappointment in the results of the meetings, but soon the same spirit that had been manifested elsewhere began to appear, and the whole city was stirred by the movement.

In Birmingham, on the first day of the meetings, the Town Hall, seating five thousand, was packed with auditors morning and afternoon, and at night Bingley Hall, which could accommodate twelve thousand, was besieged by a crowd which not only filled the building, but could have filled it many times over. During the two weeks of their stay the interest continued, and the evangelists faced larger audiences than had ever before gathered in the city. Nearly two thousand professed conversion.

In planning for the meetings in Liverpool it was discovered that there was no auditorium in the city capable of accommodating the crowds which were likely to attend. There was erected, therefore, a temporary structure, Victoria Hall, capable of seating ten thousand persons, the first structure of the kind to be erected during the work of Mr. Moody in Great Britain.

The climax of his campaign, however, was reached

THE FAMOUS EVANGELIST

in London. He had been reluctant to attempt meetings in the great metropolis, but at last consented. The most careful and extensive preparations were made. In order to reach the population spread over so vast an area, four different centres of operation were selected in widely separated sections of the city. For North London the use of the great Agricultural Hall was secured. In the East End, on Bow Road, a temporary structure was erected, carpeted with sawdust and furnished with nine thousand cane-seated chairs. The meetings in the fashionable West End of London were held in the Royal Opera House, and in South London Camberwell Hall was erected for the use of the evangelists.

The first meeting was held in the great Agricultural Hall; seventeen thousand people were admitted, and thousands were turned away from the doors. For four consecutive months the enthusiasm continued unabated. Mr. Moody preached not only daily, but often three and four times a day, indeed, quite commonly he addressed two vast audiences in widely separated parts of the city on the same evening, driving rapidly from one place of meeting to the other. Some two hundred and eighty-five meetings were held, with an estimated attendance of two million, five hundred and eighty thousand people. The city of London experienced a revival of religious interest such as never before was known, and by the widely circulated reports of the public press and of countless visitors the influences of the movement were extended throughout the United Kingdom.

Among the many results of the extraordinary services rendered during the two years which closed with the campaign in London, the following have been noted: Thousands of persons were led to enter the Christian life, other thousands of nominal church members were enabled to learn the reality of religious experience; ministers of all denominations forgot their differences and cordially co-operated in the common effort of leading souls to accept the lordship of Christ; a new and surprising interest was taken in Bible study and in expository preaching; permanent evangelistic and philanthropic institutions were established; new life was infused into all departments of church work, and singing was given more due recognition in the worship of God. These results, according to those best qualified to judge, made a deep and permanent impression upon the spiritual life of Great Britain.

VI

AMERICAN CAMPAIGNS

WHEN Moody and Sankey returned to America after their notable campaign in Great Britain there is little doubt that their names were the best known of any two men's in the world. The American papers for nearly two years had been filled with accounts of their success, and many American travellers had visited the meetings in London and in different parts of England. Consequently, from all sections of the country urgent invitations were extended to conduct series of meetings. Not only were the masses moved with an eager curiosity to see the famous evangelists, but there was a deep conviction in the hearts of many Christians that God was ready, through these accredited agents, to accomplish in America such a work of grace as had been wrought in the British Isles.

The chief difficulties confronting Mr. Moody were to select among the invitations, and to find buildings large enough to accommodate the crowds which wished to attend the meetings.

The first campaign was held in Brooklyn. Here, on Clermont Avenue, a rink capable of seating six thousand was prepared for the services. A chorus of two hundred and fifty voices was organized to lead the music. The co-operation of practically all the evangelical churches was secured. From the first the building was thronged, and that, too, in spite of an extraordinary schedule of meetings. This was as follows: Preaching every day in the week at 8:00 A. M. and 7:30 P. M.; the morning service followed by a meeting for women; a Bible reading each afternoon; a meeting for young men after the evening service. To this must be added the " inquiry meetings " held in neighbouring churches. The daily attendance upon these gatherings was estimated at more than fifteen thousand.

The result was not so much the securing of new converts as the awakening of professed Christians. Mr. Moody made clear to all, the theory on which he ever sought to promote a spiritual revival; namely, the necessity of attempting to reach and persuade individuals to become followers of Christ. As he said to Henry Ward Beecher, " There is no use attempting to make a deep and lasting effect on masses of people, but every effort should be put forth on the individual." No matter how vast the crowds with which he was dealing, this is the principle upon which Mr. Moody always worked.

Philadelphia was the scene of the second great campaign in America. The characteristic feature of the peculiarly successful meetings there was the leading part taken in them by laymen, prominent among whom was John Wanamaker. He was already well acquainted with the famous evangelist. Both men had begun their careers as Sunday school and Christian Association workers. Wanamaker was the first man to devote all his time as salaried secretary of a Young Men's Christian Association, and he established the largest and best known Sunday school in the world. He had often met Mr. Moody at Association and Sunday school conventions. He was in England and had led a noon meeting for the evangelist during the London campaign, and was abroad when arrangements were begun for the great Philadelphia mission.

In his recent life of John Wanamaker, Dr. Herbert Adams Gibbons writes as follows:

"A bit of cardboard, faded and very much worn, was one of John Wanamaker's most prized possessions. It was his usher's card at the Moody and Sankey meetings which were held in the Pennsylvania Railroad Freight Station from November 21, 1875, to January 21, 1876. No memory of his crowded life was more precious to the great merchant than this revival. No event had a more far-reaching effect upon his business and religious activities, always so closely interwoven. The great revival was held on his property, and the ushering was largely done by salesmen from Oak Hall, each of whom gave three evenings a week to this work."

Wanamaker was in Europe when a committee of Philadelphia business men, headed by Joshua L. Bailey, George H. Stuart and Alexander Whilldin, decided to invite Moody and Sankey to conduct a revival in Philadelphia. Casting around for a place large enough to hold the meetings, they hit upon the freight depot of the Pennsylvania Railroad, which was not being used. When they approached the Pennsylvania officials they discovered to their astonishment that John Wanamaker had an option on the property. They cabled him. He replied that he was soon leaving for home, and was heart and soul in any plan they decided upon. He arrived from Liverpool at the end of September, completed the purchase of the buildings and yard, and immediately turned the property over to the committee.

Not only did he offer it rent free, but he took an active part in arranging the great shed for the meetings. The tracks were taken up and a board floor put down. A great platform rising in tiers was erected at the end of the shed, and entrances were arranged on Market Street and Thirteenth Street. Stuart ordered all the chairs that the building could hold, 8,900 for the main floor, and 1,300 for the platform.

"Add eight more to the order, and we'll squeeze them in somehow," said Wanamaker.

"Why?" answered Stuart, puzzled over this request.

"Exact numbers always make a bigger impression than round numbers," was Wanamaker's reason. "If we tell the newspapers that we have 8,904 for the audience and 1,304 for the speakers and choir, people will remember the figures."

Forty thousand dollars was raised, and a generous part of it went into advertising. Sankey was John F. Keene's guest, and Moody was entertained in the Wanamaker home. All the expenses of the evangelists were met by these two men. A piano dealer, William G. Fischer, who, like Sankey, was writing hymns that were to live, gathered and drilled a volunteer choir of three hundred members.

Moody arrived some days before the opening, and gathered together some of the leading men in Philadelphia who had consented to be the workers in the aisles, watching for converts and leading them to the front. An amusing incident is related in connection with the effort of Mr. Moody to train a group of prominent business men for this work. He insisted that no one should endeavour to lead souls to Christ unless certain of his own salvation. "Are you ready to meet God?" he asked abruptly of one in the circle. "Are *you* ready?" he asked of another. The situation was growing a little too tense. He turned to Wanamaker, "Are you ready?" "Yes; ready-made," replied the

AMERICAN CAMPAIGNS

famous merchant, whose advertisements of ready-made clothing had made him famous. Both men had a keen sense of humour. The tension was relieved.

Dr. Gibbons continues: " The Moody and Sankey meetings were unique in the annals of Philadelphia. From the very first day there was a tremendous pressure for tickets, and rain or shine, for two months, weekdays and Sundays crowds found their way to Thirteenth and Market Streets the like of which had never before been seen in the city. The street-car lines revised their schedules and put on extra cars to take care of the traffic. Straight through the Christmas holidays the audiences kept coming. It was distinctively a laymen's movement, in which virtually all men of note participated. So thoroughly stirred was the community that the judges of the Supreme Court attended in a body, and President Grant and most of the Cabinet came from Washington, as guests of George W. Childs, to hear Moody preach and Sankey sing."

The total attendance at the meetings during the nine weeks was estimated at nine hundred thousand. As a thank offering a sum of nearly $127,000 was contributed; almost the entire amount was given to the Young Men's Christian Association to complete its new building in time for the Centennial Exposition which opened a few months later. Mr. Moody is quoted as saying that in all his experiences thus far he had never known any series of meetings so satisfactory in character and results as those held in Philadelphia.

However, the campaign which opened the following month in New York City was even more extensive in its preparations and in the number of persons concerned. The invitation had been extended to Mr. Moody while he was still in England. A general committee had been appointed, consisting of thirty clergymen and as many laymen representing all the evangelical churches. Special prayer services had been held for weeks in advance. As a place of meeting the Hippodrome had been engaged, an enormous structure on Madison Avenue on the site of which the Madison Square Garden was subsequently erected. Five hundred ushers were ready for service, and a choir of twelve hundred singers had been trained to assist Mr. Sankey with the music.

At the first meeting seven thousand persons were admitted to the main hall, four thousand others crowded into the overflow meeting in the smaller auditorium, and thousands were still in the streets clamouring for admission. Twenty-five thousand persons were in attendance at the various services held on the first Sunday, nor was there the slightest diminution of interest during all the following ten weeks of continuous services.

The results accomplished by the great meetings in Philadelphia and New York cannot be estimated or tabulated; but during the remaining twenty-five years of his wide ministry Mr. Moody found in practically every city he visited men who had confessed their faith in Christ for the first time either in the old freight station in Philadelphia or the Hippodrome in New York; and the wide reports of these meetings made Mr. Moody, beyond all question, the most famous religious worker of the world.

Invitations were pressed upon him from all directions. He preached in Augusta, Nashville, Louisville, St. Louis and Kansas City, but the most notable series of services undertaken before the close of the year was that held in Chicago.

MR. MOODY AT THE AGE OF 45

AMERICAN CAMPAIGNS

This city had been the scene of Mr. Moody's early labours; for twenty years it had been his home; he had the confidence of the ministers, and he was known by most of the residents; but could he succeed in drawing the crowds? Would not the very fact that everyone knew him or thought they knew him make less probable the curiosity and the sense of novelty which at first drew the throngs in other cities? Would not the prophet be without honour among his own people?

These questions were asked quite seriously even by the Christians who during a period of months were collecting money and erecting a substantial structure for the use of the evangelist in the business centre of the city. There were seats for eight thousand, and standing room for two thousand more. However, when at eight o'clock on Sunday morning, October first, the great structure was crowded to the doors and again at three in the afternoon, fears and questionings gave place to wonder and thanksgiving.

For nearly four months in this, his "home town," Mr. Moody continued to address these vast audiences, night after night, and three times on Sundays, at eight in the morning, at four, and at eight in the evening. Nor were these meetings in the tabernacle the only ones held. Twice every day Farwell Hall, with a seating capacity of twenty-five hundred, was filled to overflowing. At noon the crowds gathered to spend an hour chiefly in prayer, and again at three to listen to Mr. Moody as he gave a Bible reading. Besides these main gatherings a meeting for men and another for women were held daily. Nor was the interest confined to Chicago. The awakening was so widespread that Mr. Moody sent his helpers, in response to invitations, to many of the chief centres throughout the entire North-west; and the noon-day meeting at Farwell Hall was thrilled again and again by reports coming in by telegram of the work being done in these outlying cities.

From Chicago Mr. Moody turned to Massachusetts, the state of his birth, and to Boston, the place of his conversion when in boyhood; to Boston, against which some had warned the evangelist as being the seat of culture, the city of eloquent and learned divines, the centre of distracting religious cults and fads.

However, all warnings were unnecessary. Mr. Moody was warmly welcomed, and soon gathered about him a host of enthusiastic supporters and friends. The substantial tabernacle of brick, erected specially for the meetings, and seating six thousand persons, was filled daily to its capacity during all the weeks of the winter; and, according to the estimate of Dr. Joseph Cook, then Boston's most famous preacher, the results of the revival were even more remarkable than those under Whitefield the century before.

These five great campaigns, in Brooklyn, Philadelphia, New York, Chicago and Boston, so firmly established Mr. Moody in the confidence of the Church that invitations poured in upon him continually from every quarter. During the remaining twenty years of his life he visited the great cities and larger towns in every part of America. In San Francisco, as in St. Louis and Baltimore, he remained during a period of five or six months, in each place making a fervent evangelistic appeal and enlisting Christians in Bible study and in various forms of active service. His reputation continued to widen, so that he became beyond all question, for the century in which he lived, the most famous evangelist on earth.

VII

SUBSEQUENT VISITS TO GREAT BRITAIN

ONE convincing proof of the substantial and satisfactory character of the work done by Mr. Moody is found in the fact that he was always urged to return for further services in places once visited; and a surprising demonstration of his power consists in the further fact that these second visits were attended by success. In the case of a first campaign the sense of novelty and the desire to gratify curiosity do much to attract the crowds; but on the occasion of a second series of meetings in the same place these elements are lacking, and if great numbers assemble it is probably because they are receiving something they highly value.

Because of the abiding influence of the great work done in 1873-75, repeated invitations had been extended to Mr. Moody to return to Great Britain, and in the fall of 1881 he began a second extensive tour, so similar to the first that many persons confuse them in memory. In fact, frequent references to the life of the great evangelist would indicate the mistaken idea that he conducted only one wide campaign in the British Isles. However, in 1881-84 he visited most of the same cities, and in practically the identical order as eight years previously, and the extraordinary fact is that the interest and the results were as great and in many instances greater than before.

The work was begun at Newcastle-on-Tyne, where

the first marked success had been attained in '73. A six-weeks' mission was held in Edinburgh, and five full months were devoted to Glasgow and its vicinity.

A specially enjoyable summer was spent in visiting the smaller centres of Scotland, where Mr. Moody felt relieved from the strain of the more taxing engagements in the larger cities. Mr. Stebbins took the place of Mr. Sankey during these weeks, and they were accompanied by Professor Henry Drummond, who had rendered memorable service during Mr. Moody's former visit to Scotland, and who had then just completed his *Natural Law in the Spiritual World*.

Invitations from all parts of Great Britain became almost bewildering. Mr. Moody held a conference in London with seventy representatives of competing cities and agreed upon a program for the year which was faithfully carried out. It included the cities of southern England, and of Wales; a month in Ireland; meetings in Birmingham, Leicester and Nottingham; and two weeks each in Manchester, Leeds and Liverpool.

Before undertaking the great closing campaign in London, Mr. Moody returned to America for a summer of work in Northfield.

One of the most interesting and historic episodes of the year was the visit of Mr. Moody to the great Universities of Cambridge and Oxford, in the fall of 1882. The students of both universities showed the absurd self-consciousness and the manly chivalry which quite commonly characterize college undergraduates. They had invited the evangelists and made proper preparation for the meetings; but when their guests appeared the students were overcome by the sense of their own superiority to their uncultured American guests.

SUBSEQUENT VISITS TO GREAT BRITAIN

At Cambridge they jeered at Mr. Sankey's first solo, and then howled for an encore. They shouted, "Hear, Hear!" in response to the prayers; they interrupted the reading of the Scripture, and frequently drowned out Mr. Moody's address by chaffing questions and absurd noises. However, of the twenty-five hundred present some four hundred remained for a brief prayer service at the close of this first meeting.

The second meeting was even more discouraging, as only one hundred men were present. These men, however, were in earnest, and they realized that Mr. Moody was likewise. By Thursday night the tide had turned. The attendance greatly increased, and at the close of the service scores of students courageously took their stand in public for Christ. On Sunday night eighteen hundred men listened in breathless stillness to a message on "The Gospel of Christ," and one hundred and sixty-two gave their names at the after-meeting as desirous of knowing more of the power of this Gospel. The noon meeting for prayer, then established, has continued without interruption for nearly half a century.

The experience at Oxford was almost identical. The crowd at the first meeting overflowed the Corn Exchange. The students began to interrupt Mr. Moody, but were silenced by a sharp rebuke. On the second night they repeated their disorder, and on the third "the meeting was reduced to a hubbub, the singing and the speaking of the evangelists being interspersed with opprobrious epithets and personalities." Mr. Moody paused, and then said with grim calmness:

"We came to this city expecting to meet the flower of British gentry. I put it to you, gentlemen: Have you treated us strangers with ordinary courtesy? Whatever you may think of us and our message, we demand that you should behave at least as gentlemen toward us."

The effect was magical. He had appealed to their manhood and their pride, and when such an appeal reaches the hearts of a college audience there is always a chivalrous response. The remainder of the address was received with respectful silence. At the close a group came forward to apologize. Mr. Moody insisted that they should show their sincerity by attending the meeting the next night and occupying the front row of seats. This they did, and Mr. Moody explained the situation to the audience. His victory was complete. At the end of the address he said:

"I am much obliged to you, gentlemen, for giving me a hearing. There are thirty or forty of you here who promised me you'd come tonight and listen fair, and you've done it. I am much obliged."

From that time forward the attention accorded to the evangelists was respectful, and even eager. The audience so greatly increased that it became necessary to secure the Town Hall for the meetings; and by the end of the week large numbers of the students had made, for the first time in their lives, a public declaration of their allegiance to Christ. At the last service Mr. Moody stated that two of the happiest weeks of his life were those he had spent in Cambridge and Oxford, especially among the undergraduates, for he realized the infinite possibilities that lay in their lives. He charged them to consecrate themselves to the service of the Master; to seek, as he was seeking, for the souls of men; to have good courage, knowing in whose hands they were.

It was in the fall of the year 1883 that Mr. Moody

SUBSEQUENT VISITS TO GREAT BRITAIN 69

began his second historic campaign in the city of London. Even greater preparations had been made than for the meetings of 1875. In order that the vast population of the city might be given an opportunity to attend, two iron and wood structures were erected, and when the series of meetings conducted in the first structure was ended the building was taken down and erected in another centre. By this process meetings were held without interruption for periods of three weeks each, in eleven different districts of London. Each of these tabernacles had a seating capacity of five thousand. During the entire campaign Mr. Moody spoke to crowded halls always twice and frequently five times a day. It was estimated that during his mission Mr. Moody addressed more than two million people. The meetings had continued for the better part of a year, and were concluded with a great conference for Christian workers held from June 17th to 19th. At this time a communion service was held in which thousands from many different denominations took part.

Meetings in a single city, continuing so many months and attended by more definite results, can probably be paralleled by no campaign in the entire history of Christian evangelism.

It might be supposed that after such long years of services Great Britain would have felt that enough had been heard from evangelists in general and possibly from Mr. Moody in particular. On the contrary, at the Northfield Conference in the summer of 1891 an invitation was received which, in form at least, was the most remarkable ever received by a Gospel preacher.

It was in the form of a scroll, one hundred and fifty feet long, containing twenty-five hundred signatures, representing fifty different cities and towns and all the churches of Scotland.

This invitation having been accepted, more than one hundred centres were visited from November to March, on an average three meetings a day being held. The series closed with a mission in Edinburgh. In the spring of 1892 Mr. Moody enjoyed a two-months' trip to Palestine, and experienced the nearest approach to a vacation that he had ever known. Yet on his return to Great Britain he again plunged into work with his usual vigour, holding meetings in various places, and conducting an especially strenuous campaign in Ireland. For possibly the first time he began to show signs of fatigue, and during a series of services at Spurgeon's Tabernacle he nearly lost the use of his voice. Being persuaded to consult the famous physician, Sir Andrew Clark, he learned of an irregularity in his heart action and was cautioned as to work and diet.

"How many times a day are you in the habit of speaking?" inquired the doctor.

"Oh, I usually preach three times a day."

"How many days in the week?"

"Five days of the week, and on Sunday four or five times."

"You're a fool, sir! You're killing yourself," was the brusque response.

"Well, doctor," said Mr. Moody, "I take Saturday to rest. But may I ask how many hours a day you work?"

"Oh, I work sixteen or seventeen."

"How many days a week?"

"Every day, sir; every day."

"Then, doctor, I think you're a bigger fool than I am, and you'll kill yourself first."

SUBSEQUENT VISITS TO GREAT BRITAIN 71

With this humourous exchange the men separated, the physician ending his career within a year, Mr. Moody continuing his for seven more, but now with the knowledge that his summons might come at any hour.

On his way home to America he encountered the most thrilling and terrifying experience of his life as a passenger on board the ill-fated steamship "Spree," which suffered a broken shaft when a thousand miles from Queenstown. Water poured in through an opening in the hull. The pumps proved useless. The ship seemed to be sinking; and for days the voyagers were facing imminent death. Even when sighted by the "Lake Huron," and when being towed back toward Ireland, every hour was dark with peril. Through all these days Mr. Moody proved to be a source of help and encouragement to the terrified passengers. His service in the dining saloon instead of inspiring fear helped to bring calm to their distracted minds, and after seven days of keenest anxiety a service of thanksgiving was held in the Queenstown harbour. The conduct of the great evangelist had been like that of Paul when in the storm on the Mediterranean. It had demonstrated the reality of his faith, and had illustrated the influence of Christian heroism. The issue was for him an even stronger confidence in the Lord, whose he was and whom he served.

He reached home on the "Etruria," thus completing his visits to Great Britain, where his repeated evangelistic services during twenty years had been so signally blessed of God.

What those services meant to an entire nation is intimated by the testimony of Dr. J. Stuart Holden, of London:

" It is but bare truth to say that every class in the

community was influenced by Mr. Moody's work in Great Britain, and that about every form of Christian activity and enterprise received a divine quickening under his ministry. America may know and rightly honour Moody the educator. As such he is entirely unknown in England. It is Moody the evangelist, first, last and altogether, whose name is loved and revered. It is doubtful, indeed, if his educational schemes would ever have aroused interest in the peoples of Great Britain. They have their own. But his flaming evangelism, his zeal for souls, his transparent honesty, his loyalty to God's Word, his passion for exalting Christ, these endeared him to thousands to whom he will always stand for the best things of their Christian experience, and their children's after them."

VIII

FINISHING HIS COURSE

IN spite of his brilliant achievements in Great Britain, extending over such long periods of time, the work in his own land ever held first place in the heart of the evangelist. Nor was he a prophet without honour in his own country, for until the time of his death he continued to be recognized as the foremost evangelist of America.

It is true that in the later years of his life he found it necessary to devote an increasing portion of his time to the support of his Northfield schools; but until the very last his chief occupation was that of a Gospel herald, and as he finished his course he was still pressing the golden trumpet to his lips.

It may be that no one series of meetings equalled in popular interest the first campaigns held in 1875-77, directly after his first historic tour of the British Isles, but others of as much importance were undertaken. These are less famous probably because their character and their results were so closely identical with those previously reported.

In the winter of 1879-80 six entire months were spent in the city of St. Louis. The following winter was devoted to a strenuous campaign on the Pacific Coast. The spiritual conditions reported at the time of his arrival were serious enough to have daunted the heart of a less courageous worker. However, after five months of continuous services in San Francisco the churches were aroused to new life, large accessions were made to their membership, and pastors were given new heart for their difficult tasks, and found many fresh recruits ready to help them in all forms of Christian activity. The most signal service rendered by Mr. Moody for the city at this time was the raising of funds to meet the heavy debt resting on the Christian Association, and the consequent enlargement and advancement of the work among young men.

After an absence of three years in Great Britain Mr. Moody devoted the main portion of 1884-85 and of 1885-86 to services in many of the smaller American cities. Selecting groups of cities in different centres of the land, he would spend two or three days in each place, preaching three times daily and devoting the remainder of his time to conversations with inquirers. Usually other evangelists preceded and also followed him, so that the periods of special effort were further prolonged and the impress on the communities deepened.

In 1890, and again in 1896, great meetings were held in the city of New York. At the latter time the services were held in Cooper Union, where crowds of people were addressed each day during November and December. In 1895 services were held for several weeks in Atlanta, at a time when the Exposition was attracting to the city many thousands of visitors. The opening months of 1897 were spent in Boston, where again the messages were welcomed by great audiences representing all classes of the population. During the last year of his life, 1899, Mr. Moody again travelled on evangelistic missions as far as the Pacific Coast.

The most memorable meetings conducted during these closing years, nevertheless, in many respects the

FINISHING HIS COURSE

most remarkable he ever conducted, were those which were held at the time of the World's Fair in Chicago in 1893.

Mr. Moody never waited for crowds to come to him; he always went after the crowds; and whenever he knew that men were to gather in great numbers, there he came with his message of Christ. As soon as he heard of the plans for the Columbian Exposition, which was to attract thousands of visitors, he began planning for a great evangelistic effort to be undertaken in the city at the same time. He believed that he saw " the opportunity of a century."

While still in England he was perfecting his plans for the serious work to be undertaken in Chicago. When aboard the ill-fated steamer " Spree," on his way home, this work was specially on his heart. " On that dark night, the first night of the accident," he declared, " I made a vow that if God would spare my life and bring me back to America, I would come to Chicago, and at the World's Fair preach the Gospel with all the power He would give me."

Whether or not Mr. Moody ever preached the Gospel with greater power than during that memorable summer, it is certain that at no time did he exhibit more superb daring, or superior abilities of generalship. There was a splendid audacity in the venture itself. A summer season is usually regarded as a hopeless time for religious services in a city, and Chicago at its best was supposed to have on Sunday countless counter attractions; moreover, now every Sunday the gates of the widely-advertised World's Exposition were to be kept open, and it was certain to be the goal of the thousands who were streaming into the city from every quarter of the globe.

Mr. Moody summoned to his assistance an army of Christian workers. Evangelists and evangelistic singers were called from every part of America and Europe. In order to address the great audiences of Germans and French, Poles and Bohemians, men were employed who could speak and sing in those languages.

The Chicago Bible Institute ("The Moody Institute") was the headquarters for the campaign. Here the workers gathered every evening, and for several hours on Mondays, for conference and prayer. Mr. Moody listened intently to reports from all the meetings, and shaped plans and policies in accordance with the information received.

The first meeting was held on a Sunday in May in the Chicago Avenue Church, which was known from its founder as "Moody's Church." The evangelist spoke on "The Elder Brother of the Prodigal Son," and of the contrasted sympathy for wandering souls that should fill the hearts of Christians. The church was thronged, and likewise in the afternoon and evening. The work was extended by securing church buildings in various parts of the city, many of which buildings would otherwise have been closed during the summer season. Later on theatres were rented, and finally Tattersall's, which had a capacity of fifteen thousand and was being used for a huge military tournament, and also Forepaugh's Circus tent, which seated eighteen thousand. The big tent was secured for two Sunday mornings, and on both occasions was crowded, whereas the Sunday afternoon and evening entertainments given by the circus were so poorly attended that they had to be abandoned.

Five tents were employed and placed in unchurched communities. Two Gospel wagons were used in dis-

FINISHING HIS COURSE

tributing tracts and in holding out-of-door services. A store was rented in the centre of the city and transformed into a mission hall. Especially in the vicinity of the Fair grounds, where no churches had been erected, use was made of tents and tabernacles and the parlours of hotels.

All these vast and varied services were under the personal supervision of Mr. Moody, and upon him rested the responsibility not only of leading all the army of workers, but also of securing funds to meet all the expenses of the work. At times the latter amounted to as much as eight hundred dollars a day.

To this tremendous strain upon his strength and his resources Mr. Moody proved quite equal. The imposing campaign continued for six months, and instead of losing in intensity and spirit it gained force and interest and power as the season drew to its close. At one of the last meetings, Mr. Moody is quoted as saying:

"I thank God that I am living in Chicago today. These have been the happiest moments of my life. What a work He has given us today; what encouragements He has given us, how He has blessed us!"

At the close of the campaign, when questioned as to its results he replied: "The principal result of our six months' work is that millions have heard the simple Gospel preached by some of the most gifted preachers in the world; thousands have apparently been genuinely converted to Christ, and Christians all over this land have been brought to a deeper spiritual life and aroused to more active Christian effort for the salvation of others."

The last public appearance of Dwight L. Moody was in Kansas City, Missouri, on Thursday night,

November 16th, 1899. A typical campaign was in progress. It had opened auspiciously the previous Sunday with fifteen thousand people crowding the large Convention Hall. All the churches had united in extending an invitation to the evangelist, and around him were gathered all the religious forces of the city. All the expenses had been guaranteed, and a great chorus choir was leading the singing under the direction of Professor C. C. Case.

Mr. Moody was not well, but he betrayed no signs of weakness until at the close of each address, when he confessed unusual fatigue; but after the service on Wednesday night he appeared to be completely exhausted. He rallied sufficient strength, however, to speak in the afternoon as well as on the evening of Thursday.

If he had been told that these were to be the last services of his life, he could probably have chosen no more pertinent themes or have made more impressive appeals. In the afternoon, just before he spoke on "The Grace of God," he had Professor Case sing Fanny Crosby's hymn, "Some Day the Silver Chord Will Break," with its familiar refrain:

> "*Then I shall see Him, face to face,
> And tell the story, Saved by grace!*"

In the evening he spoke on "Excuses," narrating the parable of "The Great Supper." He closed with this characteristic appeal:

"Suppose we should write out tonight this excuse, how would it sound? 'To the King of Heaven: While sitting in Convention Hall, Kansas City, Missouri, November 16, 1899, I received a very pressing invitation from one of Your servants to be present at the

FINISHING HIS COURSE

marriage supper of Your only begotten Son. I pray Thee have me excused.' Would you sign that? . . . Just let me write out another answer. ' To the King of Heaven: While sitting in Convention Hall, Kansas City, Missouri, November 16, 1899, I received a pressing invitation from one of Your messengers to be present at the marriage supper of Your only begotten Son. I hasten to reply: By the grace of God I will be present.' "

With these words upon his lips, and facing an audience of fifteen thousand souls, the great herald of Christ ended his career. Forbidden by a physician to continue the services, he hastened to Northfield. It was the only time in forty years that he had been unable to complete a projected campaign; but his work was finished. Reaching his home, he at first seemed to gain strength; but the end was near. On December twenty-second, surrounded by his family, he fell asleep. Among the last words which fell from his lips, the following have been quoted frequently:

" Earth recedes! Heaven opens before me! . . . It it beautiful. It is like a trance. If this is death, it is sweet. There is no valley here. God is calling me! I must go. . . . This is my triumph; this is my coronation day! I have been looking forward to it for years."

That had come true of which he had spoken long before: " Some day you will read in the papers that D. L. Moody, of East Northfield, is dead," he had said. " Don't you believe a word of it! At that moment I shall be more alive than I am now. I shall have gone up higher, that is all—out of this old clay tenement into a house that is immortal; a body that death cannot touch, that sin cannot taint, a body fashioned like unto His glorious body. I was born of the flesh in 1837. I was born of the Spirit in 1856. That which is born of the flesh may die. That which is born of the Spirit will live forever."

His body was laid to rest, December twenty-sixth, on Round Top, the place which was possibly dearer to him than any other, the place where he had said he should like to be standing should he live until his Lord returned. Surely he had " fought a good fight," he had finished his course, he had " kept the faith;" surely there was laid up for him that " crown of righteousness " which the " Lord will give " him " at that day! "

IX

THE TRANSFORMING MESSAGE

WHAT, then, was the message this herald proclaimed? What was the exhaustless theme by which thousands were attracted to the same place day after day during periods of many months?

It was, in brief, the Good News of God's redeeming grace in Christ Jesus. The chief content of Mr. Moody's preaching was the love of God. It must not be supposed, however, that he failed to rebuke sin or to proclaim punishment.

A sermon which he preached again and again was from this text: " Be not deceived; God is not mocked; for whatsoever a man soweth, that shall he also reap! For he that soweth to his flesh shall of the flesh reap corruption; but he that soweth to the Spirit shall of the Spirit reap life everlasting;" and he would insist that the reaping must be of the same kind as the sowing; that a man reaps more than he sows, and that the reaping is not only in this life but in the life to come; and then he would have Mr. Sankey sing the searching hymn:

> "*Gathered in time or eternity,*
> *Sure, ah sure, will the harvest be.*"

Yes, Mr. Moody could call men to repentance quite as truly as did John the Baptist; however, his message was usually pitched to this major key: " Behold, I bring you glad tidings of great joy."

He understood his ministry to be like that of his Master: " The Spirit of the Lord is upon me, because he hath anointed me to preach the gospel to the poor, he hath sent me to heal the broken-hearted, to preach deliverance to the captives, and recovering of sight to the blind, to set at liberty them that are bruised, to preach the acceptable year of the Lord."

He found his themes always just where the Master found the words he quoted, on this occasion; namely, in the sacred Scriptures. Mr. Moody was a preacher of the Bible. It is to this fact that his success is largely attributed. He spoke of Bible characters, of Bible parables, of Bible incidents, of Bible truths. He was saturated with the teachings of the Scriptures, and he was ever seeking to make others read and study and teach the Bible. His last specific message given to ministers, at Kansas City, just before his death, urged them to open and preach the Bible. His little book entitled, *Pleasure and Profit in Bible Study,* is simply a collection of addresses he often delivered on this theme. He prefaces it by saying:

" It is always a pleasure for me to speak on the subject of this volume. I think I would rather preach about the Word of God than anything else except the love of God; because I believe it is the best thing in the world."

Or, to quote words which fell from his lips:

" We cannot overestimate the importance of a thorough familiarity with the Bible. I try to lose no opportunity of urging people by every means in my power to the constant study of this wonderful Book. People are running to religious meetings, and they think the meetings are going to do the work. But if these don't bring you into closer contact with the Word of God,

MR. MOODY ON THE PLATFORM

THE TRANSFORMING MESSAGE 83

the whole impression will be gone in three months. The more you love the Scriptures, the firmer will be your faith.

"Do you ask: How can I get in love with the Bible?

"Arouse yourself to the study of it, ask God's assistance and He will assuredly help you!

"If we feed on the Word, it will be so easy then to speak to others; and not only that, but we shall be growing in grace all the while, and others will take notice of our walk and conversation. So few grow because so few study.

"Study the Bible carefully and prayerfully.

"When the Holy Spirit touches the eyes of your understanding and you see Christ shining through the pages of the Bible, it becomes a new book to you.

"As soon as a man or woman sees Christ as the chiefest among ten thousand, the Bible becomes the revelation of the Father's love and assumes a never-ending charm."

Of course, there are many divergent views held by those who seek to interpret the Bible. Yet whatever critical theories have been advanced, and in spite of the divisions of Christians which are defended by Scripture quotations, the Bible is in reality the same body of literature it has always been, and as to its essential truths the great mass of Christians are agreed. Just because his message was so Biblical, Mr. Moody was heard with gladness by Methodists and Baptists and Presbyterians and Roman Catholics and Plymouth Brethren, and by all others who hold in common the great verities of the Christian faith. Probably no two of his hearers would have accepted all his interpretations or would have agreed in the exact statements of their own beliefs; but all felt instinctively that the Bible contained a divine message for their souls, and that they were listening to a man who was seeking to discover and to proclaim that message with passion and with power.

Mr. Moody's preaching was not only Biblical, but it was positive. With negations he had little to do. He avoided religious controversy, and believed it did more harm than good. He made great affirmations and set them forth with deep conviction, but he spent little time in dealing with those who differed.

In the last year of his life, when declining an invitation to Scotland, he said:

" The work in my own country has never been so promising as it is now. Destructive theology on the one side and the no less evil spirit of extreme intolerance on the other side have wrought wide dissensions in many communities in America. Instead of fighting error by the emphasis of truth, there has been too much splitting of hairs, and too often an unchristian spirit of bitterness. This has frequently resulted in depleted churches, and has opened the way for the entrance of still greater errors."

Mr. Moody was seeking to save souls, and he knew that controversialists do not usually win followers for Christ or encourage others to study the Bible.

In the next place, his message was vivid and picturesque. He made large use of anecdote and illustration. These were gathered from a wide field, but more commonly they came from one of two sources, either from his own experience or from some incident of Scripture. The former were not infrequently told with a touch of humour. They were usually simple and homely, often reminiscent of his early years in Chicago, of his experience with soldiers during the war, or of his dealings with inquirers in connection with his wide evangelistic itineration.

He possessed a vivid imagination, yet endeavoured to confine himself to facts, and to avoid the peril which besets many public speakers who repeat frequently illustrations drawn from their own lives. He specifically made this claim of veracity when issuing a volume of his anecdotes and illustrations.

Imagination need not make one fanciful or inaccurate; in fact, it is a gift which alone can enable one to reproduce reality. It enables a speaker to see the thing he is endeavouring to make his auditors see, and unless he sees it they never will. It enables him, further, to select the right illustration to emphasize and clarify the truth he is presenting. Particularly is it helpful in doing what Mr. Moody could do so strikingly; namely, make Bible scenes real and vivid, and cause Bible characters to live in the minds of his hearers. This colourful imagination and this skillful use of simple illustrations were among the chief factors which gave to Mr. Moody's preaching such a tremendous popular appeal.

Then again, his message was vital. He never dealt with abstractions. He did not appear to be defending dogmas, but to be deeply concerned with life. His discussions were intensely practical. He dealt with the experiences of every day. He described human joys and sorrows, and temptations and sins, and hopes and fears; and taught men and women how these could be met, and how all the experiences of time can be viewed in the light of eternity.

He was intensely human, and he spoke as one who

was consciously addressing human beings. He understood, therefore, the place not only of humour but of pathos, in public address. He realized that the head can often be reached best by an appeal to the heart. He was seeking to secure in each hearer the surrender of his will, and he knew this could be secured not only by illumining the intellect but by stirring the emotions. Yet there was nothing merely sentimental in his addresses. Their prevailing notes were downright sincerity and absolute reality, and this made them throb with vitality and pulsate with life.

Thus, also, they were urgent. As just intimated, they were in the form of appeals. The speaker was always seeking to secure decisions for Christ. This was what made Mr. Moody a great " evangelist " in the popular modern use of the word. Technically speaking an evangelist, in the New Testament sense of the term, is a man who goes to unevangelized regions; he is a " foreign missionary;" he goes as did " Philip the Evangelist," to places where Christ is not known. In this sense Mr. Moody was not an evangelist at all. He confined his work to the great centres of the chief Christian nations of the world, and worked in and with organized churches and in co-operation with ordained ministers.

Yet in a true sense he was an evangelist, and the greatest of his century; for the word has a present usage in describing one who is seeking to lead men to an immediate surrender of their lives to Christ. They work in Christian communities, but whether addressing the unchurched or members of Christian households, they are always pleading for decisions.

This was an essential characteristic of Mr. Moody's

message. "Now is the accepted time, now is the day of salvation," was his appeal. He made men feel the peril of delay, and spoke as though each service might be the last opportunity his hearers would enjoy for accepting Christ and His great salvation. Frequently his appeals would close in the spirit if not with the words, of the hymn, "Almost Persuaded," written and sung by the beloved friend of his early ministry, P. P. Bliss:

> "' Almost' can not avail;
> 'Almost' is but to fail!
> Sad, sad that bitter wail.
> 'Almost'—but lost!"

His message was a familiar message. In its substance it was wholly lacking in novelty. It was what is known as the "Old, old story"—a story ever surprisingly new to the awakened soul when conscious of its need and of the riches of grace in Christ Jesus. It told of sin and repentance, of pardon and a new birth, of victory over temptation and the attainment of holiness, of service, and of the life eternal.

He saw no reason why men should seek for a new Gospel. He believed that there were ever new adaptations and applications of the Glad Tidings contained in the Bible, but he felt that, in its essence, what men call "the old time religion" was "good enough" for him.

"Why should I get a new remedy for sin," he would ask, "when I have found one that has never failed? The Gospel has stood the test for eighteen centuries. I know what it will do for sin-sick souls. I have tried its power for forty years."

Yet his message was familiar in another sense. It

was moulded in forms which were borrowed frequently from other men. No one would dream of accusing Mr. Moody of plagiarism. Everything he touched he stamped with a character which made it his own. Yet no speaker ever seized more eagerly upon any material, from any source, which he felt would make his message more appealing and forceful. He always carried a notebook, and he would jot down any phrase, any illustration, any sermon outline, which he thought could be of use, and he had no compunctions of conscience in repeating them when occasion offered.

In speaking of his early ministry one of his biographers remarks: " He reckoned all sermons and addresses which he heard or read as so much lawful plunder. Of this he made no secret. He would sometimes say to a minister: ' I heard you preach from such a text, at such a time, and I went home and preached that same sermon to my people.' He found a discourse in a little tract entitled *Quench Not the Spirit,* and he preached it with such telling effect that twenty persons were converted by it."

In his later years, at the Northfield Conferences, he was always alert to adopt any statement which he regarded as of special value. In a company of teachers, one day, he called upon one after another by name to give a " nugget," the " best thing you have written down in your Bible." In turn he called upon L. W. Munhall.

" What nuggets have you? "

" I have some," replied the evangelist with a twinkle in his eye, " but I hesitate to give them."

" Why? " inquired Mr. Moody. " Let's have them! "

" No," insisted Munhall with a smile, " if I should,

you would take them down and repeat them in one of your great meetings, and then the next time I used them I would be accused of stealing from Moody."

"Well, then," replied Mr. Moody, greatly amused, "let some brother now speak who is not so much afraid for his reputation."

Mr. Moody is quoted as saying on another occasion: "When I get hold of a man who is versed in the Word of God, I just pump him. It is a great privilege to have the thoughts that these men have been digging for all their lives."

Yet these statements must not be misinterpreted. Mr. Moody did not repeat a thought or a phrase until it had been incorporated into his own thinking, and unless he employed it in a connection which made it original and unique.

There is, however, an added aspect of his message in view of which it can be described as "familiar." That is, his very sermons became widely known. As the years moved on he was accustomed to repeat them again and again. "No sermon is worth much," he is quoted as saying, "until it has been preached at least fifty times."

The message which opened his final campaign in Kansas City had been heard scores of times in all parts of this country and of Great Britain; and the last address he delivered had been used in outline and in substance during his first campaign in Scotland a quarter of a century before.

However, each sermon was "born again" as it was delivered. So much depended upon the personality of the speaker, so easily did he adapt each address to the occasion, so much of freshness was there in the emphasis and the phrasing, that one could read a printed sermon of Mr. Moody's and the very next hour hear Mr. Moody preach that sermon, and could listen with profit and delight.

Most of all, the message of Dwight L. Moody was a Christian message. This may sound like a truism or a platitude; it is in fact the most important characteristic of his preaching. It cannot be said of all preachers that the centre and sum of their preaching is Jesus Christ. That could be said of Moody.

If you had asked him whether he believed in the " divinity of Christ," he might have replied as did Beecher: " Why, I do not believe in anything else." So absolutely had he yielded himself to that divine Being, so ardently did he seek to bring others into fellowship with Him, that he could say truthfully of all his evangelistic career: " For to me to live is Christ." He had no doubts as to the deity of his Lord; and always argued that if Christ was not God then his followers must be guilty of breaking the first Commandment, for they " worship Christ as God."

In the truest sense his message centred in the atoning work of Christ. He preached " Jesus Christ and him crucified." Yet he did not fall into the error of preaching a dead Christ, nor into the more subtle error of urging men to seek salvation by putting their trust in a dogma relative to the death of Christ. He taught men to have faith in a Person, and not in a doctrine. He proclaimed a living Christ. His message began at the cross, but never ended there. The Gospel he preached told how " Christ died for our sins according to the Scriptures; and that he was buried, and that he rose again the third day according to the Scriptures."

His definite aim was to persuade men to yield themselves in obedience to this living Lord and in all things to do His holy will. He pled with men to forsake sin, and he promised victory to all who looked to Christ for help.

However, he entertained no illusions as to the higher life. He owed much to the teachings of C. H. Macintosh, and to his *Notes on Scripture*, in which the distinction is clearly drawn between the " standing " and the " state " of a Christian.

He knew the joy of pardon. He knew what it was to be " accepted in the Beloved." He believed that " there is now therefore no condemnation to them that are in Christ Jesus." Yet he did not think that he had " been made perfect." He believed in a " new birth," but that this is but the beginning of an ever developing spiritual experience.

He did not believe that the " old nature " or " the flesh " was dead, or " quiescent," or inactive. He knew that the Christian life was a continual conflict; that " the flesh lusteth against the spirit and the spirit against the flesh," so that we may not do the things that we would.

He urged men to live " the overcoming life," yet he taught them that " the old Adam never dies; it remains corrupt," and to illustrate the activity and power and peril of the old appetites and tendencies and passions, even in the truest Christian, he told the story of the gentleman in India who got a tiger cub and tamed it so that it became a pet. " One day when it was grown up it tasted blood, and the old tiger-nature flashed out, and it had to be killed. So with the old nature in the believer. It never dies, though it is subdued; and unless he is watchful and prayerful, it will gain the upper hand, and rush him into sin." So, he taught that through all this mortal life the old nature will remain, and will continually strive for mastery, and will need to be subdued; but he knew what it was to return thanks to God " who giveth us the victory through our Lord Jesus Christ."

The only point as to which the teachings of Mr. Moody were said to diverge from the common body of Christian belief were as to his interpretation of prophecy. Yet the most careful scrutiny of his sermons can discover little in this connection that is extravagant or fanciful or absurd. In fact, his utterances were peculiarly restrained and Scriptural. As to the return of Christ he simply affirmed with the Church of all the ages: " He sitteth on the right hand of God the Father Almighty, from thence He shall come to judge the quick and the dead. . . . I believe in . . . the resurrection of the body and the life everlasting."

He was called a " pre-millennialist " because he did not affirm that a " millennium " of peace and righteousness must intervene between this present age and the coming of Christ.

He taught that no one knew when Christ would return. He never set any dates for Christ's appearing. He announced no elaborate program of future events. He did not discuss the " millennium," nor the details of Christ's predicted reign. He always taught that the return of Christ might occur within the lifetime of any Christian, that it was the " blessed hope " of the Church, since with it were associated the resurrection of the dead, reunion with loved ones, and blessings for the whole world.

Again and again, from the time of his first visit to Scotland, he discoursed upon "heaven;" but his

THE TRANSFORMING MESSAGE 93

famous sermon is remarkably free from all crass materialism and exuberant flights of fancy. It is rather a sane and sober setting forth of the reality of a future life, with its essential experiences of fellowship with Christ and the attainment of likeness to Him.

The message of Mr. Moody was a plain presentation of the great Christian verities, and it is largely summed up in the familiar lines of another famous evangelist, J. Wilbur Chapman:

> " *Living, He loved me; dying, He saved me;*
>   *Buried, He carried my sins far away;*
> *Risen, He justifies freely forever;*
>   *Some day He's coming: Oh, glorious day!* "

X

METHODS WHICH SECURED SUCCESS

THE most important fact in relation to one who comes as a herald of God concerns the message he is sent to deliver. When that message is one which falls from many other lips and is, in substance, familiar to all who hear, it must be of interest to inquire also why, in any particular case, pre-eminent success is attained and peculiar interest aroused.

It can be affirmed of Mr. Moody that the remarkable results of his ministry were not due to miracle or mystery or chance. There was, of course, as a supreme factor the operation of the Spirit of God. The evangelist was called to do a special work at a particular time, and he was merely the human instrument which God employed. His career is not to be explained by his ancestry, nor was he merely the product of his times. He was a divinely chosen agent for a specific task. However, the Spirit of God works according to definite laws. There is always a human side to every great spiritual movement. What, then, were the methods which Mr. Moody employed?

It should be said, then, that his campaigns were usually planned with the forethought of a great general, and that every detail was carried out under his personal supervision.

First of all, specific preparation was made. Not only were Christians united in definite seasons of prayer in various churches, but there was established

METHODS WHICH SECURED SUCCESS

a noon-day meeting at some central point, and this meeting was continued during the whole series of services. Prayer, in the mind of Mr. Moody, was not a mere convention to be properly observed in connection with religious gatherings; it was an actual power by which results could be obtained. Therefore at these noon-day meetings definite petitions were presented, reports of the work were given, and a spirit of belief and of expectancy was aroused. Thus the entire campaign was conducted in an atmosphere of prayer.

Then, too, special services were often held in a town or city for considerable periods of time previous to the arrival of the evangelist, just as it was also true that such services were frequently continued after his departure. In such services great help was rendered by such speakers as Henry Drummond, Major D. W. Whittle, Dr. L. W. Munhall, Dr. George F. Pentecost, and such singers as P. P. Bliss, George Stebbins and James McGranahan.

Great care was exercised in providing a place of meeting. When necessary, special buildings were erected. These were well lighted and heated and ventilated. Mr. Moody was always deeply concerned about the comfort of his audience. In the midst of a sermon he would stop to say: "Will the ushers please open the windows? Fresh air is as important as the sermon. We must keep these people awake, and they are half asleep already." Soon people were seen shrinking from the draught; and then the windows were ordered to be shut, but possibly to be ordered open again.

Still, Mr. Moody did not welcome interruption; yet he knew how to announce a hymn and to resume his discourse when an interruption occurred. He was a master of assemblies, and no one knew better how to conduct an opening service so as to prepare the audience for a sermon. He was always in command, and announced hymns, read Scripture, had seasons of prayer, made brief remarks, called for solos, until the minds of the great crowds were fused into one, focused upon the speaker and ready to listen to every word he should utter.

A corps of ushers was always appointed and carefully instructed as to their duties; and large bodies of workers were enlisted, ready to give spiritual help to inquirers who might be aroused by the message.

Huge chorus choirs were frequently organized, and drilled. Few men realized more fully than did Mr. Moody the tremendous influence of music upon a popular gathering, and he used the musical parts of the services with telling effect.

The services were well advertised. This was usually achieved, in the daily press, by the very prominence and space given in the papers to reports of the meetings. Yet many other methods were employed to keep the meetings continually in the mind of the public.

In making all these arrangements Mr. Moody was aided greatly by laymen. These were often very prominent men of affairs without whom the impressive results of the meetings never could have been attained. These business men devoted themselves day and night during long periods of weeks to all the plans and problems of these ambitious campaigns. Nothing was left to chance. Nothing was done carelessly, and in no small degree the success of Mr. Moody was due to the enterprise and sagacity and fidelity of a numerous group of influential men who, in England and in America, were loyal supporters of his work.

His method of preparing sermons was rather original, yet not wholly unfamiliar to preachers in these days of filing-cabinets and other similar devices. He would take a large envelope, and write on the outside the subject or text; for instance, " Excuses," or " Sowing and Reaping," or " Daniel." Then he would use this envelope as a storehouse into which he would slip any outline or illustration or sentiment bearing upon the particular theme.

As to the " secret " of his sermon-making he said: " I have no secret; I study more by subjects than I do by texts. If, when I am reading, I meet a good thing on any of these subjects, I slip it into the right envelope and let it lie there. I always carry a notebook, and if I hear anything in a sermon that will throw light on that subject, I put it down. Perhaps I let it lie for a year or more. When I want a sermon I take everything that has been accumulating. Between what I find there and the results of my own study I have material enough. Then, I am all the time going over my sermons, taking out a little here and adding a little there. In that way they never get very old."

Thus each sermon became a treasure house in which a wealth of material was accumulating. Before speaking, he would take one of these envelopes, run through its contents, and select such items as he felt would be helpful for the particular address. He would arrange the main ideas in some logical order, and select anecdotes or other illustrations to give life and colour to each successive point. He would then write out with large letters certain main headings and phrases, and put these in the leaves of his Bible to refresh his memory, if at all necessary, during the delivery of his address.

Thus, while his speaking was in a sense extempore, it

was following a definite plan and order of thought, and while his sermons were frequently repeated, they usually had in them something fresh and novel either in substance or order.

In the delivery of his sermons Mr. Moody was surprisingly natural and conversational. He seemed to be talking to the persons in the third or fourth row of seats, but he spoke with such distinctness as to be heard by fifteen or twenty thousand people, and this at times in the open air. His voice was not rich, nor did it seem to be particularly strong, but his lungs had great capacity, and he was able to project his tones without apparent effort.

His language was extremely simple, made up of strong, crisp Anglo-Saxon words and phrases, which were acquired, in large measure, by his long familiarity with the English Bible.

His utterance was very rapid, frequently at the rate of more than two hundred words to the minute, which is nearly twice the speed of most speakers. As in the case of Phillips Brooks, from the very moment he began speaking the attention of the auditors was arrested by a perfect torrent of words and images and appeals and vivid metaphors. Because of his rapidity of utterance an occasional slip of the tongue, as " done " for " did," " come " for " came," was hardly noticed, nor the characteristic colloquial " aint," and " 'taint," " comin' " and " goin'," nor the frequent dropping of syllables.

He never seemed to have time to give to Daniel more consideration than " Dan'l," and Israel was always " Isr'el." Even as to the pronunciation of Jerusalem, Dr. Pentecost remarked in public: " Anyone who can pronounce Jerusalem in two syllables can do almost anything." Of this remark considerable notice was taken by the press of England, and it called forth Spurgeon's characteristic comment:

"I thank God there is one man in such hot haste to get the Gospel to the people that he does not stop to pronounce all the syllables of every word."

Not only because of the simplicity of his language, but because of their pictures and stories, his messages could be understood and appreciated by the least tutored and the youngest of his hearers.

He had a fine sense of humour, which often pervaded much of his discourse. He never seemed to use it, however, to amuse or entertain the audience, but to make some truth more real, or its presentation more acceptable and impressive.

In no less degree did he possess the power of pathos. His anecdotes were usually homely incidents drawn from common life, but they touched the heart-strings of the people, and prepared the way for his call to action or belief.

Yet the supreme quality of his delivery was his earnestness. He was straightforward, free from all attempt at elegance in phrase or diction, and always was moved by intense moral passion.

There was nothing perfunctory, stilted, or artificial in his manner. There was not usually much variety of gesture, yet there was withal a very real eloquence. He could make his hearers see the picture he was painting, whether it was Elijah ascending in his chariot of fire, or Daniel in the den of lions, or Jesus transfigured on the mount. Everything was intensely real, whether he was describing the death of a little child or the return of the Prodigal Son.

Then, also, the message was always kindly and sympathetic. Passion in public speech often partakes of harshness, of severity, or bitterness. Moody made men feel that he loved them; and he did love them. That was the secret of his power, if there was any secret. He approached his audience with a tender heart, and no matter how severely he might denounce sin or how faithfully he might warn against punishment, he was obviously and always seeking the good of his hearers and sympathizing with them in their weakness and their need. He always appeared to have in mind the familiar words which many eloquent earnest defenders of the faith seem to forget: "Though I speak with the tongues of men and of angels and have not love, I am become as a sounding brass or a tinkling cymbal."

The unique feature in the evangelistic campaigns conducted by Mr. Moody was the use of the "Inquiry Room." This was no chance expedient, but a method of work in accordance with the genius of the evangelist and with the consuming passion of his life. It afforded opportunity for him and his assistants to have private conversations with persons who wished spiritual help and guidance, especially with those whose interest had been aroused by any particular service.

When a building was erected for the use of his meetings, a room was always constructed behind or beneath or near the speaker's platform, and to this room at the close of each address all persons were invited who wished to meet Mr. Moody or his helpers.

During the singing of a hymn these persons were urged to come forward, to the Inquiry Room, before the congregation had been dismissed. It was explained that their coming would not commit them to any definite course of action, but would give them an opportunity for further considering the subject which had been discussed or for receiving some help in solving their spiritual problems. By having the Inquiry Room at the front of the building, and by giving an opportunity for those who desired to enter before the congregation was dismissed, the danger was avoided of having those who were interested swept out of the building by the crowds who surged towards the doors when the benediction was pronounced.

In case the building used in the campaign had no room which could be thus employed, a neighbouring church or hall was appointed to serve the purpose.

On entering the Inquiry Room Mr. Moody would at times announce a hymn or deliver a short address, but his time was spent almost entirely in personal conversations with those who had become concerned as to their spiritual welfare. Meanwhile other workers busied themselves with individuals, seeking to bring them to definite decisions and to a full surrender to Christ. The amount of nervous energy which Mr. Moody would expend in these after-meetings and intimate interviews was astonishing, especially when these hours of labour were being devoted by one who was delivering two or three or even four addresses to vast audiences the same day.

This exhausting toil was an expression of the deepest convictions of his soul; namely, that public proclamation of the truth does not fulfil all the responsibility of the Christian worker, but that he must deal face to face with anyone who can be persuaded to talk about Christ; and, further, that if a spirit of inquiry or a new interest has been aroused in any auditor by an evangelistic appeal, then, that very hour, avoiding the danger of delay, a definite committment to Christ should be made.

At first this use of an Inquiry Room was criticized and regarded with suspicion, particularly at the beginning of the first campaign in Scotland; but the results were so satisfactory that it soon became recognized as one of the most wise and helpful methods which Mr. Moody had introduced. Not only were doubts removed, and serious questions answered, but acquaintanceships were formed between inquirers and Christian pastors and other workers, so that those who made an intelligent decision to begin a new life were brought into the fellowship of Christian churches; and thus the results of the evangelistic services were made definite and permanent.

The life of Mr. Moody has no more important message for the present day than is found in his insistence that it is the privilege and duty of every professing Christian to exert definite personal influence toward bringing others into a vital relationship with Christ and into membership with his church.

The only difficulty Mr. Moody had in connection with the Inquiry Room was that of finding a sufficient number of men and women able and willing to speak concerning spiritual matters, or to state clearly the most simple Christian truths to those by whom the Inquiry Rooms were being crowded day after day.

The financial methods of Mr. Moody were sometimes questioned, as is the case with most successful evangelists, but never has there been less ground for criticism. There is no special reason why pastors and evangelists should be expected to take vows of poverty —or celibacy. Some may voluntarily assume the latter, but the Christian public usually sees to it that the former is unnecessary. If a few religious workers are excepted and remunerated for their toil, they should not be blamed. Other Christians are rich and are not rebuked, but are honoured as " stewards of the Lord."

Possibly some evangelists, in matters of finance, may have employed methods not above suspicion; surely Mr. Moody never did. He was on no salary, had no guarantee for any services, and accepted whatever the committees conducting his campaigns might wish to give. He lived simply, educated his family, provided for his wife, and died with only $500 to his credit. Even that balance was unknown to him. His executors found it in the form of a mortgage which had been drawn in his name by a man he once had befriended.

It is true that thousands and thousands of dollars passed through his hands; he had a legal and a moral right to retain large sums; but everything was used immediately for some benevolent or educational or evangelistic purpose.

He believed in immediate investments. Whether in the use of money or talents or time or friends, his one purpose was to make Christ real and regnant in the lives of men. He adopted any proper method and accepted every possible opportunity which promised to accomplish that one great end.

XI

THE GOSPEL IN SONG

IT is a surprising fact that a man who could not sing, who, indeed, could not distinguish one tune from another, set more people singing and gave a wider circulation to sacred songs than any musician or composer of his age. This Mr. Moody did by enlisting and encouraging leaders and writers of hymns, by gathering huge audiences of people to whom their compositions could be taught, and by publishing and circulating books which carried their words and melodies to all the lands of the world.

It is true that some people of refined taste and unquestioned ability do refer with disdain to " Gospel Hymns " as embodying poor poetry and worse music. As to such hymns, however, two or three facts must be borne in mind. The first is that obviously all hymns of this class are not of equal merit. Some do embody mawkish sentiment, and have no more melody than a " tinkling cymbal," yet others convey true sentiment, and will remain as permanent additions to the hymnology of the Christian Church.

Then, again, the world needs to learn that music in itself is not necessarily either elevating or inspiring or ennobling; everything depends upon the ideas which are associated with the sounds. Music stirs the emotions more quickly and more deeply than any other art, but the direction the aroused emotions take depends altogether upon the words or thoughts to which the strains have become wedded. For example, the notes of what, in the land of its birth, was but a trifling love song, bring to all English-speaking worshippers the message of ": O Sacred Head Now Wounded," and bear us to the foot of the cross. Thus the very simple and artless tune of some Gospel hymn may become a vehicle for bringing to the soul some priceless truth concerning our divine Lord.

It must be remembered, also, that sacred songs and evangelistic hymns, and all church music, belong not to the sphere of exact but of applied art, and must be appraised not by abstract standards, but by their results and by their usefulness in accomplishing desired ends.

A musical composition might be admirable when judged by the canons of pure art, but utterly useless for uniting in praise a great miscellaneous throng representing every class and creed. On the other hand, some very modest and humble hymns have embodied so much of Christian truth and have been united with such tuneful melodies that they have placed songs not only on the lips but in the hearts of thousands, and have sped on the wings of the morning to the uttermost parts of the sea.

The most famous singer associated with the work of Mr. Moody was Ira D. Sankey. He was not a professional musician, but a revenue officer, living in Newcastle, Pennsylvania, who had attained some popularity as a leader of singing in religious and political gatherings. The two men first met in 1870, at an Association Convention at Indianapolis. Mr. Moody at once recognized Mr. Sankey's ability and abruptly requested him to resign his position and assist in the mission and Association work which Mr. Moody was conducting in

Chicago. For some time the singer hesitated, but within six months he accepted the invitation and joined the man whose name henceforth was to be inseparably associated with his own.

In 1873 he accompanied Mr. Moody to Great Britain. His name was utterly unknown in the world of music; in two years he returned home as the most famous singer of the day. Under his influence a new kind of hymn had come into universal vogue, the "Gospel Hymn;" a new collection of sacred songs had been published and was being translated into twenty languages, and five million copies were being distributed on all the continents of the globe; a new order of Christian workers had come into being; namely, the "Gospel singers;" for the first time, and henceforth for two generations at least, preaching and singing evangelists were united and were going forth to their work, being given equal prominence and recognition, and sharing almost equally in the credit for results achieved.

Mr. Sankey had received no training in music or in singing; but he possessed natural gifts of a very high order. He had a baritone voice of limited compass but of unusual sympathy and volume. His interpretation of hymns and his phrasing were not always in accordance with the rules of musical art, but he always caught the spirit of the song and made its message absolutely clear to his auditors. He made it apparent that the music was not an end in itself, but always a humble means of conveying truth to the hearts and consciences of others. He sang with deep feeling and with the evident purpose of bringing conviction to the hearer.

He had learned to produce his tones so correctly, and

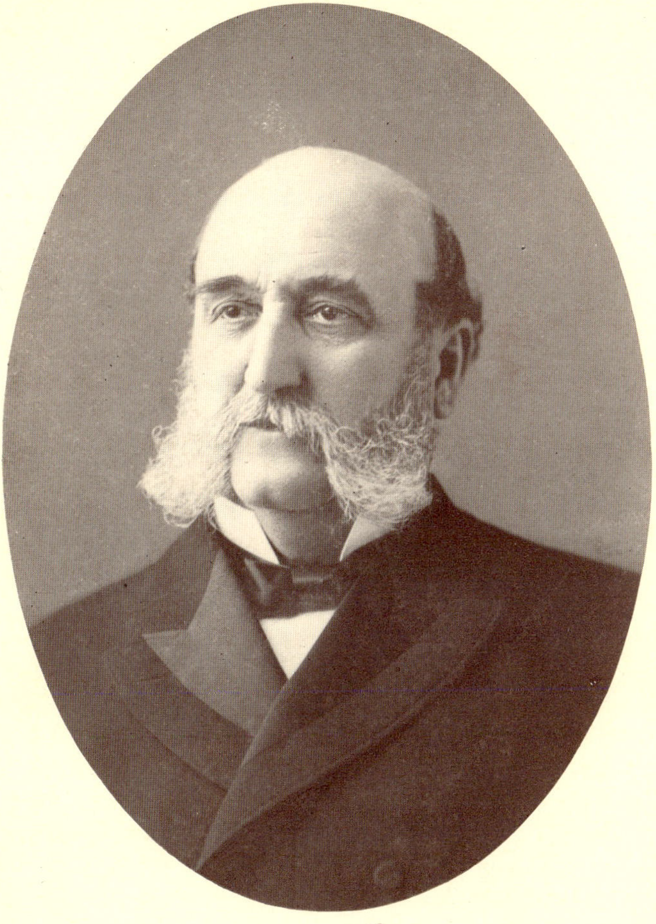

Ira D. Sankey.

THE GOSPEL IN SONG 107

he enunciated his words with such distinctness, that every syllable was heard and understood at great distances and by vast audiences. To illustrate, the following incident is related in the story of his life which came from his own pen, and is vouched for by men whose veracity there is no reason for questioning:

On a still summer evening, at an open-air service, seated on the steps of the Congregational Church at Northfield, with the front of the frame building serving as a sounding-board, he sang "The Ninety and Nine" so clearly and distinctly, and with such a volume of sound, that he was heard by a man fully one mile away, and across the Connecticut River. The man was converted by the appeal of the hymn and "lived to become an official member of the church from the steps of which the sweet song had been sung."

Mr. Sankey continued the story as follows:

"On the occasion of laying the corner-stone for the new Congregational Church in Northfield, Mr. Moody asked me to stand on the corner-stone and sing "The Ninety and Nine" without the organ accompaniment, as he hoped that this church would be one whose mission it would be to seek the lost ones. While I was singing, Mr. Caldwell, the man who had heard the song across the river, lay dying in his cottage near Mr. Moody's home. Calling his wife to his bedside, he asked her to open the south window, as he thought he heard singing. Together they listened to the same song which had been used to lead him into the way of life. In a little while he passed away to join the Shepherd in the upper fold."

It is not much less difficult to believe the statement as to the origin of this particular hymn, which also comes from Mr. Sankey himself. On their first visit to

Scotland, when travelling from Glasgow to Edinburgh with Mr. Moody, he chanced to read in an American newspaper a poem by Miss Elizabeth Clephane. He cut out the poem and put it among his hymns. The next day the evangelists were holding a meeting in the great Free Assembly Hall in Edinburgh. Mr. Moody spoke on "The Good Shepherd," and at the close of his address asked Mr. Sankey to sing a solo. On the spur of the moment the words he had read on the train came to mind. He placed them before him, seated himself at the little cabinet organ, sounded a few chords, and then sang the words to the tune which came to him spontaneously note after note. There was a solemn hush as his voice floated out over the great audience:

> *"There were ninety-and-nine that safely lay*
> *In the shelter of the fold.*
> *But one was out on the hills away,*
> *Far off from the gates of gold;*
> *Away on the mountains wild and bare,*
> *Away from the tender Shepherd's care."*

Then when he reached the great climax:

> *"There arose a glad cry to the gates of heav'n,*
> *'Rejoice, I have found my sheep.'"*

a thrill swept the vast assembly, a thrill which tens of thousands of hearts have felt since when those words have been sung and heard.

This tune is not music of a high order; it is inferior to other compositions of Mr. Sankey's; but it is an illustration of the fact that a very simple melody may be adapted to accomplish a specific purpose, and may succeed where a more perfect creation would fail. It

THE GOSPEL IN SONG

may have power enough to carry the message while being itself unnoticed, unobserved.

Until his visit to Scotland Mr. Sankey had never attempted the composition of hymns for Gospel services. His first attempt was in supplying music for the beautiful poem by Dr. Bonar, "Yet There is Room." His second hymn, "I'm Praying for You," attained immediate and immense popularity, and is still being played and sung, especially at evangelistic services, in all parts of the world.

He continued to write many hymns, some of which proved to be of wide service. Among these may be mentioned "Hiding in Thee," "Trusting Jesus, That is All, "When the Mists Have Rolled Away," "A Shelter in the Time of Storm, "While the Days Are Going By," "Under His Wings," "Faith is the Victory," and "There'll Be No Dark Valley."

He was not a great composer, he was not eminent as a leader, but as a soloist he had an almost unique gift of being able to subordinate the music and the musician while sending forth a true, clear, arresting message, and making it lodge in the hearts of his hearers. In listening to Sankey one did not think of the singer, but of the song. Thousands yielded themselves to Christ under the influence of his hymns. Many heard Moody preach because drawn by a curiosity to hear Sankey sing; many who were not moved by the preaching were affected by the singing, and vast throngs were prepared by the music for the convincing message which came in the sermon which followed.

Mr. Sankey co-operated cordially with Mr. Moody in all his plans, working with individuals in the Inquiry Rooms, enlisting the service of singers and training volunteer choirs.

He was a man of large physique, and he possessed a certain personal magnetism which gave him immediate control of large audiences. Like Mr. Moody, he had a sense of humour, and was fond of good stories. He liked to speak, and often gave " introductions " to his solos. Fearing these might become too long, Mr. Moody amused an audience, as he followed Mr. Sankey's remarks with a sermon on " Talents," urging each one to use his own, and saying: " Now, some people can preach, and others can sing. I can't sing, but I can preach; Sankey can't preach, but he can sing."

He accompanied Mr. Moody on all his great campaigns in Great Britain and on his most important missions in America. He aided in compiling and publishing volume after volume of " Gospel Hymns," which were printed and circulated by the million copies. From royalties on these books he received considerable sums of money, and he states in his biography that he erected and equipped an Association building in his home town of Newcastle, and purchased " a beautiful lot " for his " old church."

He survived Mr. Moody by nine years, but the closing period of his life was spent in physical weakness and in the night of total blindness. It was in August, 1908, that he fell asleep and caught that vision which shall be ours " when the mists have rolled away." He was by no means the first to sing or write evangelistic hymns, but he was most widely influential in making Gospel songs popular throughout the world.

Another singer whose name is inseparably linked with that of Mr. Moody was Philip Paul Bliss. He was a talented musician who also possessed poetic gifts enabling him to write both the words and the

THE GOSPEL IN SONG

music of most of the hymns which have made his name famous.

He had published two volumes of hymns before Mr. Moody became known as an evangelist, and some of his hymns were of special service to Mr. Moody on his first extended campaign in Great Britain. For instance, " Only an Armour-Bearer," proved to be the hymn which was possibly the most popular of all in that campaign. Then, again, " Free from the Law," when sung by Mr. Sankey, is said to have done more than any other one thing to overcome the prejudice existing in Scotland against Mr. Moody's message and Mr. Sankey's " kist o' whistles." In those earlier years, at least, " Daniel " was one of Mr. Moody's favourite " Bible characters," and with his sermons two hymns by Mr. Bliss came to be associated, " Dare to Be a Daniel " and " Are Your Windows Open Toward Jerusalem? " Again and again Mr. Moody would preach on " Sowing and Reaping," and just as frequently Mr. Sankey would sing, " What Shall the Harvest Be? " Mr. Moody's most moving appeals to decide for Christ were frequently strengthened when they were followed by " Almost Persuaded." Possibly the hymn by which Mr. Bliss became best known was " Hold the Fort;" yet he composed many others of probably greater artistic merit. Among his compositions might be mentioned: " More Holiness Give Me," " The Half Was Never Told," " Let the Lower Lights Be Burning," " Hallelujah, He is Risen," " Go Bury Thy Sorrow," " Pull for the Shore," " The Light of the World is Jesus," and " When Jesus Comes."

He wrote music for words by other authors, as in his beautiful tune, written for Mr. Spafford's lines, " It is well with my soul."

The full scope of Mr. Bliss' genius appeared, however, when he sang the hymns and music of his own composition. Like Mr. Sankey, he always played his own accompaniments, seated at a small cabinet organ. He was of impressive size and attractive appearance. His voice was a baritone of wide range and sympathetic quality, and was under perfect control. The special characteristic of his singing was its spiritual glow and fervour. His face was radiant with joy. No one who heard him can ever forget the pathos and the exultation which pulsated through the phrases as he sang:

> *"Bearing shame and scoffing rude,*
> *In my place condemned He stood;*
> *Sealed my pardon with His blood;*
> *Hallelujah, what a Saviour!"*

He had been serving as choirmaster and Sunday school superintendent at the church in Chicago of which the pastor was the Rev. E. P. Goodwin, D.D., a close friend and adviser of Mr. Moody. Under the influence of the evangelist he decided to devote all his time to Gospel singing. He became associated with one of Mr. Moody's fellow-workers, Major D. W. Whittle, serving as his soloist and choir leader. At the close of his Chicago campaign of 1876 Mr. Moody requested Major Whittle and Mr. Bliss to continue the evangelistic services in the city when he started for Boston. On his way to fill this appointment Mr. Bliss and his wife met their tragic death, at Ashtabula, Ohio, as the train on which they were journeying crashed through the bridge and fell seventy-five feet into the river below. His death came as a crushing blow to both Mr. Moody and to Major Whittle.

The latter was one of the most trusted and beloved evangelists of his day, and from their first meeting, as the Major returned wounded from the war, Mr. Moody held him in the warmest affection. He was, indeed, one of the most brave and tender and lovable of men. Giving up a successful business career, he devoted his life to evangelistic work. He preached a pure Gospel, fearlessly and faithfully, and was widely known for his Bible readings. Furthermore, he possessed gifts as a writer of hymns, which appeared under the assumed name of " El Nathan." The following were given very wide acceptance: " I Know Whom I Have Believed," " I Shall Be Satisfied," " Sometime We'll Understand," " There Shall Be Showers of Blessing," " The Crowning Day is Coming," for all of which hymns the music was written by James McGranahan, his associate in evangelistic work. Others of his hymns, as " Moment by Moment," were set to music by his daughter, Mrs. W. R. Moody.

For ten years following the death of Mr Bliss, Mr. McGranahan served with Major Whittle as his Gospel singer. They met first at the tragic scene in Ashtabula, where both had gone to search for some trace of Mr. Bliss, with whom each had a close friendship. Mr. McGranahan soon after determined to unite in the evangelistic work which was under the general direction of Mr. Moody. He soon began to write Gospel hymns, but his greatest service, possibly, was his association with Mr. Sankey and Mr. Stebbins in compiling the successive collections of Gospel hymns which became popularly known as the " Moody and Sankey Hymns."

The most gifted singer of those who were engaged in this special work, and one who for many years was among the most intimate and trusted of Mr. Moody's friends was Mr. George C. Stebbins. He was a trained musician, and for some time had been engaged in church work as a soloist and choir leader when he was invited by Mr. Moody to become associated with Mr. Sankey and himself in evangelistic work. His first task was to train the large choir for the Chicago campaign of 1876. During the campaign he was associated with Major Whittle in services in neighbouring cities. Under the general direction of Mr. Moody he subsequently accompanied Mr. George C. Needham, and later Dr. George F. Pentecost, as soloist and choir leader. Again and again he accompanied Mr. Moody to Great Britain, and for many years he conducted the music at the Northfield Conferences.

As Dr. L. W. Munhall, doughty defender of the faith, is the sole survivor of that group of evangelists who assisted Mr. Moody in his work in Great Britain and America, so George C. Stebbins is the only one still living of those Gospel singers who had a part in his notable campaigns. Of all those hymn-writers, his productions are still the most popular and most certain of a permanent place in the hymnology of the Church. " Saviour, Breathe an Evening Blessing," " There Is a Green Hill Far Away," " Oh, to Be Over Yonder," " Fully Trusting," " I've Found a Friend," " I Shall Be Satisfied," " Take Time to Be Holy," " Jesus, I Come," and " Tenderly Calling," are among those which have been justly popular, and which illustrate the high character of his true and melodious compositions.

Mention should also be made of Mr. D. B. Towner, who for years conducted the music for the young men's conferences at Northfield, and was engaged by the

Moody Bible Institute to train evangelistic singers. He was for years more or less under the direction of Mr. Moody, and assisted in the absence of Mr. Sankey, or worked with some of the associated evangelists. During these years he wrote many popular hymns, among which " Trust and Obey " and " Anywhere with Jesus " are possibly the best known.

It must not be supposed that Mr. Moody used no hymns excepting those composed by his immediate associates. He and Mr. Sankey, of course, employed in their meetings, and embodied in their books, scores of the grand old hymns of the Church, as well as many of the popular hymns of the day. Indeed, the song which as the result of their meetings was heard in the churches and on the streets of every American and English town and city, " The Sweet By-and-By," was a production of Bennett and Webster. Such hymns as " Ring the Bells of Heaven," " Knocking, Knocking," and " When He Cometh," are associated with the name of Dr. George F. Root; " Shall We Gather at the River? " and " Where Is My Wandering Boy To-night? " with the name of the Rev. Robert Lowry; as are also such hymns as " I Need Thee Every Hour," " Saviour, Thy Dying Love," " Marching to Zion," and " Up from the Grave He Arose."

Mr. Sankey sang very frequently and with great effect the hymn, " We Shall Meet Beyond the River," composed by Hubert P. Main, the well-known editor, publisher and collector of books of praise. He used also the hymns of Sweeney and Kirkpatrick, of W. F. Sherwin and of E. O. Excell, the soloist, leader, composer and publisher.

Yet, after all, the most prolific writer, whose Gospel hymns were given wide vogue by the Moody and

Sankey meetings, was the blind poetess, Fanny J. Crosby. The first of her compositions to become popular, " Safe in the Arms of Jesus," was followed by scores of others, varying in merit, the total at last numbering more than eight thousand. These were recorded, and large numbers of these were published by Mr. Main. Many musicians composed music for these hymns, but possibly none was of more aid in giving them wide acceptance than W. H. Doane, who wrote the music for " Jesus, Keep Me Near the Cross," " Pass Me Not, O Gentle Saviour," " Safe in the Arms of Jesus," " Hide Me, O My Saviour, Hide Me," " Rescue the Perishing," " Though Your Sins Be As Scarlet," " Draw Me Nearer," " Saviour, More Than Life to Me," and many others.

In the matter of " Gospel Hymns," therefore, Mr. Moody is not to be given the sole credit for their composition, for their circulation, for their wide popularity, or for the services of all who became Gospel singers; but the use of these productions in his extensive campaigns, the recognition and prominence he gave to those who assisted him in the service of song, and the distribution of millions of copies of these hymns in all lands, were due in largest measure to his personal influence. He gave to sacred music a new place of eminence in religious worship, and he demonstrated the fact that even simple songs could become the vehicle for conveying to human hearts the melody and transforming power of the Gospel of Christ.

XII

AN UNORDAINED PASTOR

DWIGHT L. MOODY was never ordained to the Christian ministry; he was foreordained, however, to be a Christian pastor. It is true that his experience in that rôle was confined to an early period of his life, but the story should be told here, because the church which he then established is one of those organizations by which his influence is being extended to the present day.

In his first independent effort at Christian work the youthful Yankee had invaded a forbidding section of Chicago known as " Little Hell," and there had fearlessly planted the standard of the cross. Out of a tumultuous gathering of street urchins and incipient criminals he developed a Sunday school which met in the so-called North Market Hall, and first came into being in 1858. The growth of the school was phenomenal; it soon had an enrolment of a thousand, and was exercising a marked influence on the community. Largely for the benefit of the parents of the scholars Mr. Moody established a meeting on Sunday night; and later on held evangelistic services every night in the week. It was evident that larger and better accommodations were needed. In 1864 Mr. Moody collected some $20,000 among his friends, and erected a rather ambitious structure with an auditorium seating fifteen hundred, and with rooms for various departments of Sunday school work and religious activity.

A problem arose as to what should be done with the converts who in increasing numbers were professing their faith in Christ. Mr. Moody urged them to become members of established churches, but this they were reluctant to do. They were personally attached to Mr. Moody, and preferred his informal methods and messages to the apparently less fervid and more perfunctory worship of other Christian congregations.

Consequently the determination was reached to organize a church; but what should be its form of polity and its ecclesiastical relationship? To aid in answering this question Mr. Moody called into conference his friends in the ministry and a number of prominent laymen. Practically all the evangelical denominations were represented at the meeting. After a period of prayer Mr. Moody related the history of the Mission, the success of the work, the difficulty of persuading the converts to unite with existing churches, and the desire that an orderly congregation should be formed, of which he should be pastor, and in which the ordinances of the Gospel should be observed and the preaching of the Gospel continued.

The discussion which followed was long and interesting. One by one, however, the representatives of the various denominations found it necessary to withdraw. The Episcopalian regretted that he could not recognize as a church an organization with a layman as its head. The Presbyterian was delighted with the work, but felt it should be under the care of Presbytery. The Baptist was cordial, but felt that the converts should be immersed, and regretted that the proposed pastor had merely been sprinkled. The Methodist was an ardent friend of Mr. Moody's, but he was persuaded that Mr. Moody should join the

AN UNORDAINED PASTOR

Conference, and that the spiritual condition of his followers was such as needed the stimulation of class-meetings and love-feasts, quarterly meetings and camp-meetings. Moreover, he had a lingering suspicion that there was a Calvinistic taint in some of Mr. Moody's teachings.

The Congregationalists, who alone remained, found it difficult to conceal their satisfaction that they possessed a form of church government equal to such an unusual emergency. Thus the "Illinois Street Church" was organized as an independent, self-governing church. The candidates for membership were examined and baptized by the ministers who were present, and they observed together their first communion. However, the "pastor" was not ordained; and Congregationalists never published his name in their "Minutes," nor recognized the church in their printed statistics.

Nevertheless, both "pastor" and people seemed to have been recognized by the Holy Spirit. The church building became a seething centre of Christian activity, and a scene of continual "revival." In addition to the usual church services there were meetings for men, meetings for boys, meetings for girls, meetings for mothers, meetings for strangers, meetings for Bible study, Gospel meetings, praise meetings, meetings for testimony, meetings and more meetings, in the church and in the homes of the people, and each with some distinctive feature. At each meeting Mr. Moody was sure to be present, excepting when three or four were held at the same time, in which case it may be concluded he attended one after another.

In all this multiplicity of activities he was the centre. In the increasing congregation of workers and worshippers he was the leader, the chief priest, the pope, the "pastor," call him what one may. He called himself a "deacon," a fitting New Testament title signifying "a servant;" and such indeed he was, and no "shepherd" or "pastor" was ever more ready to render to any member of his flock more self-denying service than he gave, day and night.

He knew the needs of his people. They were ever on his heart. He not only worked and worshipped with them in the church, but he visited them in their homes. On a single New Year's Day he made two hundred calls upon different members of his flock, a large proportion being "in garrets and the upper stories of high tenement houses." He used a conveyance drawn by horses, and he was accompanied by several men of the congregation, but before night the horses were exhausted, and one by one his helpers had fallen by the way; so that, to his amusement, the tireless "pastor" concluded his Marathon of ministerial visitation on foot and alone. The next New Year's Day he did without the carriage as involving needless expense, but accomplished about the same breathless round of greetings, prayers and benedictions.

As commander-in-chief of his forces he did not follow the course pursued by some pastors, either from choice or by necessity, of doing all the work of the church. He was most skilful in enlisting workers. He always insisted that it was better to set ten men to work than to do the work of ten men, and that it is never wise to do anything which you can make anyone else do even half as well.

Quite a number of his men had been trained to conduct services, even to "preach" in the absence of the "pastor," and all the members were being taught to

AN UNORDAINED PASTOR

win souls for Christ. The success of the church during the years to come was in no small measure due to the fact that it was so truly a congregation of Christian workers.

It must not be supposed that Mr. Moody assumed the duties of a pastor out of any disregard for "ordination" or with any disrespect for established churches. He simply undertook, for a time, a task which he believed had come to him in the providence of God. He never administered baptism, but had new converts baptized in other churches. He did, however, conduct communion services, and performed most of the functions of a minister.

For a time, 1866-1869, as he became more absorbed in Y. M. C. A. and evangelistic work he did have his friend, the Rev. J. H. Harwood, serve as minister; but this was more in the nature of an interregnum than the establishment of a constitutional monarchy. He again assumed control, and with the exception of those years, from the organization of the church in 1864 until the time of his great British campaign in 1873-75, D. L. Moody was the unordained pastor of the Illinois Street Independent Church.

Before the opening of that campaign, however, the church had changed its location and its name. The building had been swept away by the great Chicago fire of October, 1871. Mr. Moody had at once entered heartily upon the work of relief carried on by the Y. M. C. A. and other organizations and churches for the help of the homeless thousands who had suffered from the appalling disaster. But very soon he started east to hold evangelistic services and to collect funds for the erection of a new building. Largely through the generosity of George H. Stuart and John Wanamaker, of Philadelphia, $3,000 was placed in his hands for the erection of a temporary structure.

This was located on a site near that on which the Illinois Street Church had stood. It was built of rough boards and roofed with tar paper, and had a seating capacity of more than one thousand. This so-called North Side Tabernacle was dedicated within two months and a half after the fire, and was the first structure for religious and educational purposes to be erected in all the vast devastated region on the North Side of the city. So few people had found any place in the region where they could live that it seemed absurd to erect so large a temporary structure, but the first time that it was opened for Sunday school a thousand children were in attendance, many of them accompanied by their parents.

Excepting a short time spent in a visit to England in 1872, Mr. Moody devoted his energies ceaselessly to the work of this Mission, and made it a great centre for evangelism. He ministered both to the souls and bodies of men. Large quantities of clothing and provisions were sent to him for distribution among those who had suffered in the fire. Homeless wanderers were welcomed to the warmth and shelter of the Mission building, in which Mr. Moody himself took up his temporary residence, using for this purpose one of the smaller rooms which had been provided for the Sunday school work. Great crowds attended the services, which were held almost continuously. Children walked miles through cold and heat to attend the Sunday school. Sewing classes were conducted for girls, mothers' meetings were held, large Bible classes were conducted, particularly for women under the leadership of Miss Dryer. In his evangelistic services Mr. Moody

AN UNORDAINED PASTOR

was frequently aided by such workers as Major Whittle and Harry Moorehouse, and had to help in the Gospel singing not only Mr. Sankey, but Mr. Bliss and others who subsequently became prominent as leaders of sacred song.

A Sunday in this crude structure was a day of deep interest. The Lord's Supper was always observed at nine o'clock in the morning. The preaching service was at ten-thirty. At noon a luncheon was served in the "kitchen-dining-room" for the officers and the Sunday school teachers. After luncheon the teachers met for the study of the lesson. At three the Sunday school was held, and Mr. Moody acted as superintendent. This was followed by a teachers' prayer-meeting, also led by him. Then supper was served. This was followed by a meeting with the "Yoke-Fellows," a band of men organized to extend invitations to the services. Mr. Moody preached at eight, and then held an Inquiry Meeting, which often lasted far into the night.

Every minute of this crowded day Mr. Moody utilized to advance the work and to stimulate the workers. The large gathering around the long dining table at luncheon was used as an occasion of informal instruction and discussion. Mr. Moody would begin: "Mr. R., where did you read in the Bible this morning at the time of your devotion? What did you find there?" and the question would go around the table. "What is the best truth in the Sunday school lesson for to-day?" "How do you know you are saved?" "What would you say to a person who asked you what it means to be saved?" "What is your text for this year?"

The text which Mr. Moody had selected for 1873 was repeated by him on New Year's Sunday at this noon luncheon. In view of the plans he had formed to go to Great Britain and his extraordinary experiences there the words were significant: " For the Lord God will help me; therefore shall I not be confounded; therefore have I set my face like a flint, and I know that I shall not be ashamed " (Isaiah 50:7). He started for Great Britain intending to be absent for only a few months and then to resume his work as pastor. He had already secured a lot and large subscriptions for a permanent building to be erected on the corner of Chicago Avenue and La Salle Street. He did not return until more than two years had elapsed, and never did he resume his former relation to the church. His interest in its welfare, however, never failed.

During most of his stay abroad the work continued without any recognized leader, although Mr. Moody corresponded regularly with the members even when engaged in the absorbing work abroad. The activities somewhat flagged; the church was subjected to rather severe criticism by representatives of certain denominations. There was financial stringency, and much difficulty in collecting subscriptions for the new building. The basement was completed, a temporary roof was provided, and construction work was suspended.

At this time a committee was appointed, consisting of Major Whittle and Dr. E. P. Goodwin, to secure a pastor, whose support Mr. Moody himself guaranteed. The supremely important qualification as specified was that the pastor selected " should teach the essential truths of the Bible in unquestioned orthodoxy." He was to be a " competent interpreter of the Scriptures," and fitted to conduct a school for Christian workers which Mr. Moody hoped to establish. The selection

AN UNORDAINED PASTOR

fell upon the Rev. William J. Erdman, who began his ministry in Chicago on April 14th, 1875. Due to his college and seminary training, this first ordained pastor introduced certain new phases of life and forms of Bible teaching into the work of what now became known as the Chicago Avenue Church. This Mr. Moody, on his return to America, at once recognized and heartily approved.

The pastor was highly esteemed as a harmonizer in a congregation where he discovered rather determined " Congregationalists, Presbyterians, Methodists, Baptists and Plymouth Brethren." He was a studious and faithful teacher, and sympathetic with all forms of evangelistic and Gospel work. During his pastorate the church finally adopted its " Articles of Faith," which had been prepared by two of its members, Messrs. Watts De Golier and David Montgomery. These " Articles " are extremely simple, and consist wholly of verbatim quotations from the Bible. They posit belief in one true God, the Father, the Son and the Holy Ghost; in the Bible as given by inspiration of God; in the facts of sin and judgment and of salvation through Jesus Christ, who " died for our sins, according to the Scriptures;" in the love of God revealed by the gift of His Son, and in the possession of eternal life through faith in Him; in the fact that Christ is the Head of the Church, and that He has instituted the ordinances of Baptism and the Lord's Supper.

The Principles of Organization and Government are prefaced by the statement: " This body of believers desire to be known only as Christians, without reference to any denomination; yet regarding all who hold and preach the truth contained in our articles of faith as equally belonging to the same Head; and are thereby free to co-operate and unite with them in carrying on the work of our common Master."

During this pastorate, also, the church began its work in a completed structure. The funds necessary to finish the building were provided by the sale of Gospel hymns. It seems that at the close of the campaign in Great Britain, in 1875, Messrs. Morgan and Scott reported to the London Committee who had arranged for the Moody meetings that they had on hand $35,000 which had accrued as royalties on the "Moody and Sankey" hymn-books. The committee refused to accept the money, and insisted that it belonged to the evangelists. The latter, however, refused to accept it. Here, then, was a snug sum of money which no one would claim.

A member of the Chicago Avenue Church suggested that the money might appropriately be spent in completing the Chicago church in which Mr. Moody was so deeply interested. The admirable suggestion was acted upon. The structure was completed, and on June 1st, 1876, was dedicated, free of debt. The sermon on this occasion was preached by the Rev. James H. Brookes, D.D., of St. Louis. The building became historic as the scene of marked spiritual revivals, of faithful preaching and teaching of the Bible, and of the continuance of a Sabbath school work of vigour and wide influence.

The first pastor of the Chicago Avenue Church, Dr. Erdman, was succeeded by the Rev. Charles Morton, 1878-9; Evangelist George C. Needham, 1879-81; the Rev. Charles F. Goss, 1885-90; the Rev. R. A. Torrey, D.D., 1894-1901; the Rev. A. C. Dixon, D.D., 1906-1911; the Rev. Paul Rader, 1914-21; and the Rev. W. P. Philpott.

AN UNORDAINED PASTOR

In 1915 the need of a larger auditorium became manifest. A desirable site was purchased some distance farther north, on Clark and La Salle Streets, at North Avenue, and upon it was erected a spacious temporary tabernacle, while the building on Chicago Avenue was sold to the Moody Bible Institute.

Subsequently this tabernacle was displaced by the present structure, known as "The D. L. Moody Memorial Church and Sunday School." This remarkable building was constructed at the cost of nearly a million dollars. It is in many ways unique among the churches of America. The architect received his inspiration in part from the early Christian church of St. Sophia, Constantinople, and in part from the Romanesque churches of Italy. There is in the design a combination of massiveness and simplicity. As in St. Sophia a vast multitude worshipped in a spacious temple unimpeded by pillars, so the vaulted auditorium of this new church is wholly free from columns or other obstructions. It is provided with 2,200 seats on the main floor, and 1,840 in the balcony, and the acoustic properties are so perfect that the conversational tones of a speaker can reach all of the four thousand auditors. The Sunday school building is equipped to accommodate 2,500 scholars, and forms a harmonious unit with the main auditorium of the church.

The building was dedicated on November 8, 1925. It forms a superb monument to the memory of Mr. Moody, particularly as it is employed to carry on Christian work along the specified lines which he adopted more than half a century ago.

The "D. L. Moody Memorial" is in the truest sense a "people's church." Its congregation does not include persons of wealth. The motto from the first has been: "Ever welcome to this house of God are strangers and the poor." It is an undenominational, independent, evangelistic, missionary church. Eighty of its members are in service on the foreign field. Its thriving Sunday school makes certain a continued influence for the generation to come.

In this church Mr. Moody kept his membership as a layman during his whole life. Surely he builded better than he knew when as an unordained pastor he established that unconventional organization which now perpetuates his memory and bears his name.

XIII

A CHRISTIAN EDUCATOR

THE Moody Bible Institute, according to Miss Emma E. Dryer, is a child of the Chicago Avenue Church; in a very real sense, however, it is also a monument to the patience and persistence and fidelity of Miss Dryer herself. She was Dean of Women in the Illinois State Normal School, a woman of great ability as a teacher and organizer. At the time of the Chicago Fire she happened to be visiting friends on the West Side, the portion of the city which escaped in the great conflagration. She remained to engage in the general work of relief, particularly among the women and children. Becoming acquainted with Mr. Moody, she rendered valuable assistance as a teacher of women's Bible classes in his North Side Tabernacle. He urged her to give up her work in the Normal School and to devote all her time to Bible teaching among women. " That is good work of its kind," he insisted, " but there are teachers enough who want to teach school, and schools enough that want them; but there are not enough to do this work, and this is the best work."

Acting upon this advice, Miss Dryer began her mission in Chicago. Consulting with Mr. Moody, she undertook to train women who would visit from house to house as " Bible readers," and " city missionaries." They were to work in needy localities and in connection with the churches, and for the further instruction of such workers Mr. Moody planned to establish a training school. In 1873, called to England for his first long series of meetings, he left to Miss Dryer the conduct of the Bible work. His plan was for a school in which only women should be trained.

"What will you do for the men?" asked Miss Dryer.

"Let the theological seminaries take them," he replied; "we'd find ourselves in hot water quick if we undertook to educate young men."

Later on, however, his purpose widened. He saw the need of training laymen, not to be pastors, but to help in various forms of Christian activity and, more specifically, so to know the Bible that they could lead others to Christ by personal conversation and influence.

Nevertheless, Mr. Moody for some years was too engrossed in evangelistic work to undertake the establishment of a Bible school. Miss Dryer engaged quarters in the Y. M. C. A. building in which to conduct her "Bible Work." She secured friends for the work, prominent among whom was Mrs. Cyrus H. McCormick, whose gift of $500 was the first large contribution received. She was also greatly encouraged by the aid in Bible instruction given by Dr. Erdman, the pastor of the Chicago Avenue Church.

Mr. Moody's stay abroad had been unexpectedly prolonged, but he had not forgotten the Bible work in Chicago; on his return he requested Miss Dryer to meet him for a conference in New York, at the time of the famous Hippodrome campaign. She presented the need of a home where the Bible workers could live together and receive instruction for their task. Mr. Moody urged her to select a site, and to give him estimates of cost. She chose as a location the lots adjoining the Chicago Avenue Church, and when Mr. Moody

A CHRISTIAN EDUCATOR

visited the city for his evangelistic campaign in 1876 he examined these and other properties and approved the selection made.

He was too much engaged to undertake the task of organizing the proposed school, but he encouraged the Bible work and stated his hope that a way would be provided for training large numbers of workers, who, by house-to-house visitation and distribution of Bibles, might aid in the more complete evangelization of the city.

In 1885, as Mr. Moody was passing through Chicago, he attended a meeting of those who were interested in the Bible work, and listened to their enlarging plans. He stated that he would not undertake the leadership of the project unless $250,000 were first raised. He saw difficulties in the way, and even proposed moving the work to New York. The money, however, was soon contributed, and the following committee appointed to recommend a location for the building: Mr. John V. Farwell, Mrs. Cyrus H. McCormick, Mr. N. S. Bouton, and Miss E. Dryer. They agreed upon the site selected in 1876; but Mr. Moody still hesitated. As Major Whittle explained: " His home was now in Northfield, and it would be difficult to conduct a large work in Chicago; he already had a great many irons in the fire, he was everywhere in demand as an evangelist, and was carrying many burdens."

After a series of evangelistic services in Chicago in 1886, it was decided, with the concurrence of Mr. Moody, to re-incorporate the Bible work as " The Chicago Evangelization Society." This decision was reached at a meeting in February, 1887, and the name of the new organization was to be " The Bible Work

Institute." The object of the organization was "to educate and direct and maintain Christian workers as Bible readers, teachers and evangelists, who shall teach the Gospel in Chicago and its suburbs, especially in neglected fields."

It is very evident that Mr. Moody looked upon the project not so much as an educational as an evangelistic effort. His purpose was not to prepare a "short cut to the ministry," but to furnish lay workers for Chicago. However, for three years nothing was done toward erecting a building. In fact, the next year, when passing through the city, Mr. Moody even proposed that three homes, in three different sections of the city, should be secured for the Bible workers, instead of erecting a central building.

Meanwhile a May Institute for Bible Study had been established by Miss Dryer for the instruction of the Bible workers, and of other Christian workers who might wish to attend. The enrolment in 1886 was fifty, in the next year seventy-five; and the numbers and interest continued to increase. In 1889 Mr. Moody promised to attend; and to accommodate him the Institute was held in April, and instead of the Y. M. C. A. building the Chicago Avenue Church was used for the sessions.

Mr. Moody was surprised and delighted at the attendance, which numbered over two hundred, and he decided then and there to establish the long-considered training school. He at once contracted for the site adjoining the church. Difficulties arose, and some further delay ensued. However, a new Board was formed, of which Mr. William H. Holden, a brother-in-law of Mr. Moody, was elected president. Three dwellings to the north of the church were secured as

A CHRISTIAN EDUCATOR

dormitories for women, and the erection of a building for the use of men was begun. The services of the Rev. R. A. Torrey, of Minneapolis, were secured as superintendent of the Institute, and with a week's Bible Conference beginning September 26th, 1889, the Chicago Bible Institute began its career.

Students began to enroll in large numbers. It was arranged that all students must undertake definite work in homes and missions, in churches and on the streets, while pursuing their courses of study. The training was of a practical character.

Dr. Torrey was well prepared for the task he had undertaken. He was a university and seminary graduate, and a man of unusual evangelistic spirit and gifts.

The ten years ensuing, until the death of Mr. Moody, were marked by continual growth and expansion in the activities of the Institute. By that time the buildings and property were valued at $325,000. Students were in attendance from all quarters, and representing practically all races of the world. Hundreds had gone forth to careers of usefulness. More than two hundred were engaged in home and city and rescue missions; 186 were on the foreign field.

The courses of training included systematic study of the Bible, and instruction in various forms of Christian service. A musical department was established for those who were intending to serve in the capacity of choir leaders and Gospel singers. The students were engaged in house-to-house visitation, in conducting meetings for women, meetings for children and meetings in jails, and in every form of effort which would prepare them for efficient personal and public evangelistic activity. During these years Mr. Moody continued his deep interest in the work, directing its policies, raising money for its support, and rejoicing in its surprising success.

Since the death of Mr. Moody the Institute, which is now known as the "Moody Bible Institute of Chicago," has continued uninterruptedly its phenomenal growth. In 1905 a change was made in the by-laws of the institution, giving it a wider objective than at first proposed. According to this revision, "Its object is to educate, maintain and send forth Christian workers, Bible teachers, Gospel singers, teachers and evangelists, to preach and teach the Gospel of Jesus Christ."

The present character and success of the Institute are due largely to the influence of Dr. James M. Gray, who has served as dean since 1904, and to the efficient, generous and active leadership of Mr. Henry P. Crowell, who for more than a quarter of a century has been the President of the Board of Trustees. The Institute now occupies thirty-four buildings, with a valuation of $4,406,000. It has an enrolment of one thousand students, and in addition 700 are attending night classes, while some 7,000 persons are following the correspondence courses of Bible study. In the past twenty-seven years more than 3,500 have been graduated from the courses of study, and the correspondence school has registered 36,270 students. Missionaries who have gone to foreign fields number 1,209.

An extraordinary enterprise established by Mr. Moody and connected with the Chicago School for Christian Workers is the "Bible Institute Colportage Association." It had its origin in his conviction of the vital need of inexpensive books which would carry the Gospel message to all classes. When he tried in vain to secure reading matter for young Christians at a

A CHRISTIAN EDUCATOR

local bookstore in a Wisconsin town, he began an investigation which revealed the fact that religious books had a very limited circulation, largely because of their high prices. These prices were due to the limited number of editions. He therefore determined to select a few books which would be popular, undenominational, Scriptural, evangelical, and to print these in enormous quantities. For this purpose the Bible Institute Colportage Association was founded in 1894, in connection with the Chicago Bible Institute. The first order given was for 100,000 copies of *The Way to God*. Subsequently large editions were printed of *Heaven, Pleasure and Profit in Bible Study, The Way of Life, Prevailing Prayer*, and many similar volumes.

The experiment was an immediate success. Colporteurs carried these books into every quarter of the great cities and out into the rural districts, and were able to secure for themselves ready support by the sales. The price of each volume was but ten cents at first, the low price being made possible by the enormous numbers sold. During the remaining four years of his life Mr. Moody saw the enterprise expand until it had covered the continent and extended into countries beyond the seas. The books have been translated into a score of foreign languages, and millions of copies are in circulation. The success of the enterprise was due in large measure to the wise administration of Mr. A. P. Fitt, Mr. Moody's son-in-law, but the inception of the idea was with Mr. Moody, and to him the chief credit is due for this form of service which is bringing the Good News to countless readers in all lands.

The establishment of the Northfield and Mount Hermon Schools, even more than the Chicago Bible Institute, brought Mr. Moody into the field of education. He had attended neither a high school nor college, yet he had two admirable qualifications for an educator: he was a Christian, and he possessed common sense. Because he was a Christian he desired to secure the advantages of an education for young people by whom, without his aid, such advantages could not have been enjoyed; and he believed that the great aim of an educational institution should be the development of Christian character and preparation for Christian service.

Because of his common sense, he did not propose to open charity schools or give absolutely gratuitous instruction, but he planned to require every student to perform daily a certain amount of manual or domestic work, and to provide for at least a part of the expense of the education received. In order to secure the Christian character of the schools, he determined to make the Bible the chief textbook, and to maintain in the schools a natural but definite religious atmosphere.

To protect the independence and to preserve the self-respect of the students, each was to pay or earn at least one-half the cost of board and tuition, and each one was to work an hour every day either in the buildings or on the farm. No sooner had Mr. Moody established his home in Northfield, on his return from Great Britain in 1875, than he began to be impressed with the fact that there were many boys and girls in the rural districts, even near his own home, who were being denied the advantages of an education; and he determined to do what he could to meet their need.

The first building of what became the Northfield Seminary for girls was begun in the spring of 1879, but Mr. Moody could not wait for its erection. He

A CHRISTIAN EDUCATOR

opened the school in his own house in November, with twenty-five students, and classes were held in his dining-room until the new building was completed. Within the next twenty years he saw the Seminary expand until it had an enrolment of nearly four hundred students, a faculty of some forty teachers, a property of five hundred acres, nine domitories and a number of other buildings. Since its opening some 1,470 young women have been graduated by the Seminary.

The Mount Hermon School for boys was established in 1881 on the west bank of the Connecticut River some five miles from Northfield. At first the boys admitted were quite young, but later it was determined to receive no students under sixteen years of age. A very large proportion came to take college preparatory courses; but others, whose advantages had been more limited, were given instruction of a more general character. The caption on the school stationery is a quotation from Mr. Moody; it reads: "To help young men of limited means to get an education such as would have done me good at their age."

The ideal of helping others is that which has pervaded the life of these schools. Pupils are not admitted who are financially independent, and the purpose is to send graduates out into the world with the conviction that service is the standard of greatness.

More than 1,400 students have been graduated by Mount Hermon. The present enrolment is about 500. The Seminary students number nearly 600. The enrolment in both schools represents thirty-seven states and thirty-one countries. The continued growth and wide usefulness of these schools is to be attributed to the devoted leadership of Mr. and Mrs. W. R. Moody, and their faithful associates, among whom should be mentioned Dr. Henry F. Cutler, who has given thirty-six fruitful years to the work at Mount Hermon.

Hundreds of Northfield and Mount Hermon graduates are found on the foreign mission field, and are engaged in definite forms of religious and evangelistic work at home; and of the graduates the vast proportion are witnessing for Christ in all the various callings and walks of life.

Inseparable from the work of these schools is the thought of the great conferences of Christians conducted at Northfield by Mr. Moody, by which also he rendered a real and important service in the sphere of religious education. Here he was the instrument of giving guidance and inspiration to thousands of workers who summer after summer flocked to Northfield, not so much for rest as for instruction and new stimulus in Christian life and service.

Most of these visitors were entertained in the Seminary buildings, which were devoted to the use of the summer gatherings. These gatherings have included conferences for young men, and for young women, home missionary conferences, and foreign missionary conferences. The most notable, however, has been the " August Conference for Christian Workers." In 1880 Mr. Moody had held, in September, a " Convocation for Prayer," which was attended by more than three hundred persons. The principal speaker was the Rev. H. B. Hartzler, of Cleveland. The meetings were largely devotional, but emphasis was laid on the work of the Holy Spirit. The first " August Conference " was held the next year, and was even more largely attended. Mr. Stebbins writes: " I recall very well the

MR. MOODY IN NORTHFIELD SURROUNDINGS

MR. MOODY IN NORTHFIELD SURROUNDINGS

A CHRISTIAN EDUCATOR 139

men who took part in that first conference. Mr. Moody, Major Whittle, Dr. Brookes, of St. Louis, Dr. A. J. Gordon, of Boston, Dr. Pentecost and Dr. W. J. Erdman, Evangelists George C. Needham and L. W. Munhall, and Henry M. Moore, of Boston, were among the speakers."

Most of these speakers were leaders of the " Niagara Bible Conference," established a few years earlier, and they aided Mr. Moody in giving such a prominent place to Bible teaching that the August gathering became popularly known as the Northfield Bible Conference. Mr. Moody provided, however, for the treatment of a wide variety of themes, aiming at the deepening of the spiritual life and preparation for Christian service. At the first August conference the principal speaker was Dr. Andrew Bonar, of Scotland, and it became the custom of Mr. Moody to invite to Northfield each year some prominent Christian leaders from abroad. Among these were F. B. Meyer, H. W. Webb-Peploe, G. Campbell Morgan, George H. C. Macgregor and Andrew Murray.

During many of the conferences a meeting was held daily on Round Top for asking questions about the Bible. For the answers Mr. Moody relied chiefly upon Dr. W. J. Erdman, who he said " was better acquainted with the Bible than any other man he had met." Leading workers in city and home and foreign missions, also, were given a part in these August Conferences, and the theme of evangelism was always prominently presented. Yet possibly it is true that the chief stress was ever laid on personal religious experience and the need of complete dedication to the will of God.

Except when he was abroad, and during the Chicago Fair, Mr. Moody always presided at the conferences, and infused into the gatherings his spirit of sanity, of earnestness, and of devotion, and his enthusiasm for every effort which aims to bring souls into vital relationship with Christ.

The August Conferences, together with the other summer assemblies, are regarded by many persons as constituting one of Mr. Moody's largest contributions to the life of the Church, particularly as an educational force, imparting to thousands new views of Christian truth, deeper aspects of Christian experience, and wider visions of Christian service.

XIV

THE INFLUENCE THAT ABIDES

EVANGELISTS and mass-meeting methods of evangelism seem to have fallen on evil days. They cannot be called popular. We are told that their time has passed. The chief condemnation which rests upon them is that their results are not permanent. We are assured that when a great " campaign " with its noise and confusion and emotion has ended, nothing visible or valuable remains. " The tumult and the shouting dies;" and, noting the spiritual reaction, some persons are said to ask whether or not the " Lord God of Hosts " is " with us yet."

This criticism may be merited by some evangelists. Not all of them are perfect; some may deserve censure. Few of us in this world are faultless. Such objections to evangelists are familiar. They were brought against Mr. Moody. Even some ministers who were pastors at the time of the great meetings in Philadelphia and New York declared that their churches " reaped no benefit from the revivals."

If any persons are sceptical as to the abiding influence of D. L. Moody, however, they might have found a dramatic vindication of the man and his methods in a notable gathering held in Glasgow, Scotland, in December, 1924. The most prominent citizens were thronging St. Andrew's Hall, the largest auditorium of the city. Over the thronged meeting the Lord Provost, the chief magistrate of the city, presided.

The occasion was the celebration of the fiftieth anniversary of the evangelistic campaign conducted by Messrs. Moody and Sankey in Glasgow, in 1874. This vast throng had met to testify that after a half-century had passed the influence of the evangelists was still vital in all the benevolent, religious, philanthropic and missionary enterprises of the city.

The meeting was held under the auspices of the Glasgow United Evangelistic Association, an organization which had been formed as a consequence of the Moody campaign. It has now become the chief centre for the benevolent and missionary activities of the city. The purpose of the assemblage was to reaffirm that what George Adam Smith had stated as to the permanent results of the campaign in Scotland, after a lapse of twenty-five years, was still true of Glasgow after the passing of half a century: "It baptized crowds in the Spirit of Jesus, and opened the eyes of innumerable men and women to the reality of the great facts of repentance and conversion, to the possibility of self-control and of peace by God's Spirit. . . . The young men who came under its influence are now in middle life; and today one can point to ministers in many churches, and to laymen in charge of the municipal and social interests of almost every town who were first roused to faith and first enlisted in the cause of God and of their fellow-men by the evangelists of 1873-75."

One of the most impressive features of the meeting was a call from the platform for all those present who had been converted during Mr. Moody's Mission, fifty years ago, to rise. More than eighty responded. A further call for similar testimony on the part of those present who had been brought to Christ through the agency of the United Evangelistic Association, "not

THE INFLUENCE THAT ABIDES 143

Mr. Moody's spiritual children but grandchildren," brought nearly a thousand to their feet.

One of the speakers told of the historic evening in 1874 when, during a men's meeting at nine o'clock after the close of the evangelistic service, one hundred and one young men responded to Mr. Moody's call and for the first time took their stand for Christ. That occasion had been known ever since as the "101 night," and of that group many had been numbered among the most prominent religious workers in the city. The speaker went on to say that recently, when making a world tour, he had met a leading architect in Adelaide who proved to be one of "the 101;" in Tasmania one of the leading Christian workers he found to be another of "the 101," and that wherever news was had of members of the group they were found to be true to Christ.

Those of the group living in Glasgow had formed a Christian Union. Among other lines of activity they had conducted, every Sunday, a Free Breakfast Service where they had fed the poor and preached the Gospel. This is still being done, as during all the fifty years past. Hundreds of hopeless characters have been saved from vice and crime, and transformed into respectable citizens.

Another remarkable incident of the evening was a brief address by Sir John H. M. Graham, one of the leading business men in Scotland. He appeared on the platform on crutches and declared that he had attended the gathering contrary to the advice of his physician, but with the conviction that he could not remain away. He himself had been brought to Christ as a young man during Mr. Moody's mission in Glasgow, and subsequently had seen much of the work in other centres of the country. He told an incident which, according to the Rev. J. Stuart Holden, D.D., is reported as follows: " At a meeting in Exeter Hall, London, at which Mr. Moody was preaching, Sir John Graham was seated between Mr. Gladstone and Mr. Matthew Arnold, the former then prime minister of England, and the latter one of the most distinguished men of letters.

" At the close of this service, Mr. Gladstone turned to his two companions and said: ' I thank God that I have lived to see the day when He should bless His Church on earth by the gift of a man able to preach the Gospel of Christ as we have heard it preached this afternoon.' Arnold replied: ' Mr. Gladstone, I would give all that I have if I could only believe it.' It is difficult to find language to express the impression made by the recital of that incident in that crowded meeting, recording as it did the fact of Mr. Moody's influence in circles usually so far removed from evangelistic contact."

Other speakers told of the various lines of work conducted to this day by the Glasgow United Evangelistic Association. Among these the following are worthy of mention:

Several large halls are kept open for daily services, where the Gospel is faithfully preached.

The Noon Prayer-Meeting begun in 1874, held in the Christian Institute, is an active power for good. Here members of many Christian denominations meet for united prayer; and here, in a sense, is a " City Exchange," at which ministers, missionaries, evangelists and other Christian workers give reports, compare notes, and extend mutual help.

The Poor Children's Sabbath Dinner has likewise

THE INFLUENCE THAT ABIDES 145

been served uninterruptedly for fifty years. It has been used as a means for becoming acquainted with thousands of needy children, who, by a variety of associated agencies, have been trained for useful lives.

So, too, in 1874 under the impulse of the Moody meetings the Glasgow Poor Children's Day Refuges were begun; these continued for thirty-five years, until the work was taken over by the government and supported by civic relief funds.

Further activities for poor children were organized in the form of Homes for the Destitute, and the flourishing Fresh-Air Fortnight Scheme, which provides health and happiness to thousands upon thousands from the city slums.

Out of the Glasgow Association has come a foreign missionary enterprise which is carrying the Gospel to the " regions beyond " and sending its message to many different lands.

Special Missions have been conducted by the Association. Under its auspices the churches were united for evangelistic campaigns conducted by Moody and Sankey in 1882; by E. P. Hammond in 1885; by Dr. Pentecost in 1888; and again by Mr. Moody in 1892. As a result of the latter visit a Bible Training School, projected on lines similar to those of the Chicago Institute, was established and a building erected at the cost of nearly four hundred thousand dollars. For thirty-five years the work of this Institute has gone on, and in that time fifteen hundred men and women have been trained for home and foreign service.

Such, in brief, was the testimony borne at the anniversary meeting which was held to witness to some of the more tangible results of the Moody and Sankey campaign, which had done so much to promote the spiritual, moral and social welfare of the city of Glasgow.

It was asserted, moreover, that the work done in Glasgow was but a sample of what had been accomplished by Mr. Moody throughout all of Great Britain. Among the most remarkable results was the establishment, at the suggestion and under the leadership of Mr. Moody, of temperance restaurants for workingmen. The idea at first was ridiculed, but when acted upon met with instant success; and these establishments, all over the British Isles, have proved to be commercial enterprises not only benefitting the patrons, but proving to be the source of vast profits to the proprietors. Such, for example, was the "British Workmen's Public-House Company." Like provision was soon made for a better class of establishments, and thus grew the modern popular "tea-rooms" and the light refreshment companies, which have been such a boon to city workers of all classes, and a valuable form of investment, also.

Nor was the influence felt in only limited localities or by any one class of the community. Testimony was borne to the fact that the classic halls of Cambridge were as truly affected as were the slums of Glasgow. The Cambridge Inter-Collegiate Christian Union, it was reported, is still conducting a daily meeting for prayer, and is continuing evangelistic efforts which date their inception to the first visit of Mr. Moody to the university town. It was seriously affirmed that the influence of Mr. Moody marked a definite epoch in the religious history of Great Britain.

This Jubilee Meeting of the Glasgow United Evangelistic Association was in some particulars unique, but it is described at some length rather because it was so

THE INFLUENCE THAT ABIDES 147

similar in its character and in its testimony to the corresponding memorial meetings held in New York, in Philadelphia, in Baltimore, in Brooklyn, and in Washington, twenty-five years after Mr. Moody's campaigns in those cities; and also because so similar a witness to his continuing influence was given at the Boston meetings held in Tremont Temple in 1927 to commemorate the evangelistic services of 1877, fifty years before.

This abiding influence of Mr. Moody has been exerted in several ways: First, through the individual lives he touched and transformed; second, through the institutions he established; third, by the movements he fostered; and fourth, by the inspiration of his memory.

As to individual lives, a few examples might be named. Let the gallant Sir Wilfred Grenfell, the "beloved physician" of frozen Labrador, tell his own story, describing his experience in his second year as a medical student in London University:

"It was in my second year, 1885, that, returning from an out-patient case one night, I turned into a large tent erected in a purlieu of Shadwell, the district to which I happened to have been called. It proved to be an evangelistic meeting of the then famous Moody and Sankey. It was so new to me that when a tedious prayer-bore began a long oration, I started to leave. Suddenly the leader, who I learned afterwards was D. L. Moody, called out to the audience: 'Let us sing a hymn while our brother finishes his prayer.' His practicality interested me, and I stayed the service out. When eventually I left, it was with a determination either to make religion a real effort to do as I thought Christ would do in my place as a doctor, or frankly abandon it.

"There could have been only one issue while I still lived with a mother like mine. For she had always been my ideal of unselfish love. So I decided to make the attempt, and later went down to hear the brothers J. E. and C. T. Studd speak at some subsidiary meeting of the Moody campaign. They were natural athletes, and I felt that I could listen to them. I could not have listened to a sensuous-looking man, a man who was not a master of his own body, any more than I could to a precentor who, coming to sing the prayers at college chapel dedication, I saw get drunk on sherry which he abstracted from the banquet table just before the service. Never shall I forget, at the meeting of the Studd brothers, the audience being asked to stand up if they intended to try and follow Christ. It appeared a very sensible question to me, but I was amazed how hard I found it to stand up. At last one boy, out of a hundred or more in sailor rig from an industrial or reformatory ship on the Thames, suddenly rose. It seemed to me such a wonderfully courageous act, for I knew perfectly what it would mean to him, that I immediately found myself on my feet, and went out feeling that I had crossed the Rubicon, and must do something to prove it."

Or, turning from Labrador to China, listen to Mr. D. E. Hoste, who as General Director of the China Inland Mission has been the leader of more than a thousand missionaries labouring in all the inland provinces of the vast country. He declares that he was leading "a careless, prayerless, irreligious life" when Mr. Moody came to Brighton, England, forty-five years ago, to hold an evangelistic mission. Young Hoste was an officer in Her Majesty's service. At a theatre service, to which he had come to ridicule the speaker, a message

THE INFLUENCE THAT ABIDES

from Mr. Moody gripped his heart, and he became interested in the meetings; he yielded himself to Christ, and ultimately devoted his life to labours in the Far East.

Or, turn from China to the heart of Africa, and sit down in the grass hut at Luanza beside " Dan " Crawford, and listen to the outpouring of one of the noblest souls that ever flamed with love for Christ, as he tells you of the messenger who fifty years before brought light to his soul, and sent him as a light-bearer to the jungles of the Dark Continent: " The ' when ' is the month of May, month of my conversion long ago in Scotland. Such an occasion is unforgettable. Like a homing pigeon my old heart harks back to the entering into ' my good estate,' as Jonathan Edwards put it; and could one vivid electrifying flash of faith do it all? Yes, back to the eighties of last century I go, back to a quiet Sunday night in this very month on this very date in May. The background is Gourock, a true-blue Presbyterian village washed by the stormy Firth of Clyde. . . . So much for the background.

" Now I see in the middle distance that dear old whitewashed barn, its Gospel texts, its roughish seats, its open door. This is a conventicle witnessing loyally to the fact that to Scotland had come ' a man sent by God ' whose name was D. L. Moody. Now for the foreground—what of it? I, even I, am all the foreground there is to it. Then a young fellow; now this same old fellow writing these loyal lines with a will. Writing to say that ' tonight ' (long ago and far away), tonight climax is coming. . . . Tonight my black fourteen days of conviction of sin, are to end in endless attainment. Tonight I am crossing the line. . . . Make no mistake! But for that ' when ' in that May of long ago there would have been no May for me in Africa today."

Or, listen as one of his biographers tells us how a college student at Lake Forest attended a meeting in Chicago, uncertain as to the salvation assured by faith in Christ; how in the Inquiry Room he had a brief personal conversation with Mr. Moody which transformed his life; how then J. Wilbur Chapman went out to become a successful pastor, the Moderator of the Assembly of his great denomination, and an evangelist who was privileged to preach the Gospel on all the continents of the world.

These may be regarded as men of unusual ability; they are named, however, almost at random as representing the ranks of that great host of individuals who, by the influence of Mr. Moody, were brought into the Christian life, and of that still greater host of professed followers of Christ who because of his labours were drawn into active Christian service. How many lives were actually transformed by contact with Mr. Moody and by the power of his message, no one can compute. Personally he had a real aversion to numbering converts and to tabulating results. He is said to have replied with characteristic bluntness to a minister who asked him how many souls he had led to Christ: " I don't know anything about that, Doctor. Thank God I don't have to. I don't keep the Lamb's Book of Life."

It is safe to assume that some hundreds of thousands of conversions resulted from his preaching in Great Britain and America.

Mr. Moody's influence was made still wider and more permanent by the institutions and organizations

THE INFLUENCE THAT ABIDES 151

which owe their origin to his varied activities. "The Moody Memorial Church" is a monument to his toil and prayers, but it is only one of a hundred churches, the activity and growth of which could be directly traced to seasons of revival which attended his work. The Bible Institute has been sending out its students into domestic and foreign fields, but to its successful career can be traced other similar institutions at home and abroad. Christian Associations in all parts of this land and of Great Britain owe their spacious buildings and their widening activities to his efforts and support. "The Northfield Conferences," like the pioneer "Niagara Bible Conference," have become inspiring models for similar gatherings, and now scores of such summer conventions assemble annually in all parts of the land.

These institutions the present generation has inherited as a rich legacy; to it comes the call not only to add to their number, but to regard it as a sacred duty to rally to their support, and to continue their activities with the evangelical convictions and evangelistic zeal which animated their founder.

The influence of Mr. Moody has been continued also by the great movements he originated or promoted. The first conference of college students was held under his leadership at Mount Hermon. He had proposed a gathering of Association secretaries, but was persuaded by Luther D. Wishard to invite instead representatives of American colleges and universities. During the conference, apparently in direct answer to prayer, and in large measure because of the influence of Dr. Arthur T. Pierson, a deep interest was awakened in the foreign missionary enterprise, and one hundred men volunteered for such service. This resulted in a visitation of the colleges by Robert Wilder and John Forman, and in the organization of the Student Volunteer Movement for Foreign Missions, which has brought into active service on distant fields thousands of the choicest young men and women of America.

So successful was this first conference that it was called to meet the next year at Northfield; and during following years, with such leaders as Robert E. Speer and John R. Mott, proved to be of incalculable help to the spiritual life of the colleges and a recruiting ground for all forms of religious and philanthropic service.

In connection with the abiding influence of all these gatherings at Northfield, mention might be made of the fact that the Keswick Convention in England, which has been for many years the largest and most influential of all Christian Conventions in the land, received large accessions to its attendance as a result of the meetings conducted up and down Great Britain by Mr. Moody. Many Christian people were awakened to a desire for deeper spiritual life and found their way to Keswick, seekers and finders of the fulness of life in Christ. Mr. Moody once preached at Keswick, and was himself tremendously impressed by the spirit of the great gathering. Its wholesomeness and sanity greatly appealed to him, while its emphasis on the crown rights of the Lord Jesus Christ moved him profoundly, and encouraged him in his efforts to widen and deepen the work of the Northfield Conferences.

By the influence of Mr. Moody, likewise, wide unorganized movements have been strengthened, movements for stimulating prayer and Bible study, and for

THE INFLUENCE THAT ABIDES 153

undertaking personal work in winning individuals to Christ.

Specifically, the movement toward Christian unity owes more to him than to any one man of his generation. The immediate effect of gathering, for months at a time, in one central place of meeting, and in one common effort, men and women of every evangelical denomination may be imagined, but its ultimate results can never be measured. Those who are loyal to our divine Lord may never be made one by an attempted unanimity of belief, or uniformity of worship, or unity of organization; but they may be brought so close together by a unity of effort, as they seek to enlist followers for Christ, that they will bear to the world that witness to His divine mission for which our Saviour prayed.

The influence of Mr. Moody is being continued by the memory of his life and work. The individuals who heard his message are passing away, the institutions he established may cease to exist or may be diverted from their proper purpose, the movements he fostered may lose their force, but as long as his memory lives, men will find it easier to believe in an inspired Bible, in spiritual renewal, in divine love and in the transforming power of the Gospel of Christ. It is for those who have known him to cherish his memory and to do all that is in their power to keep this memory vivid and vital in the minds and hearts of men. In so doing they become partakers in his work.

During his lifetime many were privileged to share in his actual tasks. They should be recognized in any appraisal of his influence, or in any complete review of his life. However, their names are too numerous and the part they played was too intricate to trace here, and too varied to describe. His career could not be understood without some knowledge of his cultured and consecrated wife, who was ever his counsellor and helper; and his continuing influence is due in large measure to the co-operation and labours of his devoted family, and of his large circle of influential friends.

However, in chief measure his great work and his extraordinary achievements are due to his own singleness of purpose, to his downright sincerity, and to the reality of his personal religious experience.

Yet, above all, the permanent influence of Dwight L. Moody must be ascribed to the power of God. He was a man truly surrendered to the divine will, and such a man is always filled with the divine Spirit. His life continues in the lives of his fellow-men. His work abides.

In such a man is completely fulfilled that unfailing promise cut in the headstone of his grave on Round Top:

" He that doeth the will of God abideth forever."

BOOKS BY D. L. MOODY

Anecdotes.
Bible Characters.
Fulness of the Gospel.
Heaven.
How to Study the Bible.
Latest Sermons.
Men of the Bible.
Moody's Stories.
Notes from My Bible.
One Thousand and One Thoughts from My Library.
Overcoming Life.
Pleasure and Profit in Bible Study.
Prevailing Prayer.
Second Coming of Christ.
Secret Power.
Select Sermons.
Short Talks.
Sovereign Grace.
Sowing and Reaping.
Thoughts for the Quiet Hour.
To the Work! To the Work!
Way and the Word.
Way Home.
Way to God.
Weighed and Wanting.
Year Book.

OTHER WORKS CONSULTED

The Life of Dwight L. Moody, by W. R. Moody.
The Life and Work of Dwight L. Moody, J. Wilbur Chapman.
Dwight L. Moody, Henry Drummond.
D. L. Moody, Worker in Souls, Gamaliel Bradford.
Life of Henry Drummond, George Adam Smith.
Recollections of D. L. Moody and His Work in Britain, " J. M." (Mrs. Peter McKinnon).
Dwight L. Moody, John McDowell.
The Shorter Life of D. L. Moody, Paul D. Moody and A. P. Fitt.
D. L. Moody and His Work, W. H. Daniels.
Why God Used D. L. Moody, R. A. Torrey.
Ten Days with Moody, J. S. Ogilvie.
Lives of Moody, Sankey and Bliss, by Elias Nason.
Narrative of the Awakening, in *The British Evangelist.*
The American Evangelists, Moody and Sankey, John Hall and George H. Stuart.
George C. Stebbins: Reminiscences and Gospel Hymn Stories.
Mighty Days of Revival: R. C. Morgan, His Life and Times, G. E. Morgan.
My Life and Sacred Songs, Ira D. Sankey.
John Wanamaker, Herbert Adams Gibbons.
A Labrador Doctor: Autobiography of Wilfred Thomason Grenfell.
Henry Drummond, James Y. Simpson.

Printed in the United States of America

BIOGRAPHY AND TRAVEL

S. HALL YOUNG, D.D.
Author of "Adventures in Alaska," Etc.

Hall Young of Alaska

An Alaskan Autobiography.

Profusely Illustrated, $4.00

To have had such a teeming life as Dr. Young's would exhaust every energy of the normal human being; but to harness one's powers to the task of passing on to others its adventures and enthusiasms, in graphic chapters that make the readers able to re-live it in their own minds and souls—this sets the climax of super-achievement on Dr. Young's eighty tremendous years. Here are thrills, heart-stirrings, incitements to adventure and achievement by the score which all readers will want to make their own.

JOHN T. FARIS *Author of "Making Good," etc.*

The Alaskan Pathfinder

The Story of Sheldon Jackson. New edition. Introduction by Dr. John A. Marquis, Gen. Sec. Presbyterian Board National Missions.

Illustrated, $1.50

"Dr. Sheldon Jackson did a pioneer work in Alaska that can never be repeated and that will not need to be done again."—*Presbyterian Banner.*

W. M. DOUGLAS

Andrew Murray and His Message $1.75

"Mr. Douglas was an intimate friend of Andrew Murray. The life story of an exceedingly interesting man, told in a most interesting way. To be brought into contact with this holy man will be the rare privilege of every reader of this volume."—*Watchman Examiner.*

JAMES O. DOBSON

Saint Francis: The Little Poor Man of Assisi
$1.50

Outlines his life, his stirring experiences and his teachings, and indicates the significance of all these for the life of men and women of the twentieth century. The book has distinct educational and thought-arousing value.

The Lorenz Guide Books in Handy Form

D. E. LORENZ, Ph.D.

The New Mediterranean Traveller

New Pocket Edition. Revised to Date.

Thin paper, round corners, $5.00

The Round the World Traveller

New Pocket Edition. Revised to Date.

Thin paper, round corners, $5.00

GREAT BIBLE CHARACTERS

JAMES I. VANCE, D.D.
Author of "God's Open," "Being a Preacher," Etc.

Love Trails of the Long Ago

Love Stories of Bible Men and Women. $1.50

Some of the subjects introduced are Vashti, Eve, Zipporah, Jephthæ, Rebekah, David, Delilah and Mary of Bethlehem, and the supreme love between Jesus and all mankind. Here is an exceedingly attractive gift book, and it is also full of suggestive value to preachers, as well as to Bible readers generally.

WILLIAM P. MERRILL, D.D.
Pastor, Brick Presbyterian Church, New York

Prophets of the Dawn

Amos, Hosea, Isaiah, Micah. The Beginnings of the Religion of the Spirit. $1.50

A thoughtful and illuminating interpretation. Dr. Merrill has succeeded in making the critical Eighth Century B. C. real and full of suggestions to the crucial Twentieth Century A. D. Here is an unusually appealing volume for layman and minister alike. It is not mere history nor yet exegesis; it is rather an interpretation, invigorated by a vivid but restrained imagination that puts new vitality into the present-day understanding of Old Testament times.

ELMER E. HELMS, D.D.

Men Who Made and Marred History

Studies in Biblical Biography. $1.25

Dr. Helms' wide experience of life, of human nature and of the Bible gained during this long, varied and vigorous ministry, is abundantly reflected in these essays and addresses on great men of Bible days. "The Man Who Gave Us a Start" is Adam, of course, but who is "The Incorruptible Man," or "The Man of Iron," or "A Crooked Man Made Straight"? The series closes appropriately and glowingly with "The Man Pre-Eminent" —Jesus of Nazareth. The volume is one of power and inspiration for every Bible reader and student—minister or layman.

A NEW EDITION
AGNES SLIGH TURNBULL

Far Above Rubies

Heart Stories of Bible Women.
Second Edition. Illustrated, $2.00

Chicago Evening Post: "Here at last are Bible women revealed through the sympathetic, creative imagination of a woman, who with great dramatic sense lifts one out of the present into Bethsaida and Capernaum."